Number Twenty-six:
The Centennial Series of the Association of Former Students,
Texas A&M University

BY
ADA MOREHEAD HOLLAND

TEXAS A&M UNIVERSITY PRESS
COLLEGE STATION

Copyright © 1988 by Ada Morehead Holland
Manufactured in the United States of America
All rights reserved
First Paperback Edition

The paper used in this book meets the minimum requirements
of the American National Standard for Permanence
of Paper for Printed Library Materials, Z39.48-1984.
Binding materials have been chosen for durability.

Library of Congress Cataloging-in-Publication Data

Holland, Ada Morehead.
　Brush country woman.
　(The Centennial series of the Association of Former
Students, Texas A&M University ; no. 26)
　　Bibliography: p.
　　1. Harbison, Helen Sewell, d. 1985- .
2. Ranch life—Texas—Jim Hogg County—History—20th
century.   3. Jim Hogg County (Tex.)—Social life and
customs.   4. Ranchers—Texas—Jim Hogg County—Biography.
5. Jim Hogg County (Tex.)—Biography.   I. Title.
II. Series.
F392.J48H374   1988   976.4′48206′0924   [B]   87-27941
ISBN 0-89096-328-3 (alk. paper cloth)
ISBN 0-89096-978-7 (pbk.)

TO MY FOUR BEST FRIENDS

Charles and Claudia
Morris and Becky

O Horrid Land. O Beautiful....
There is something about the brush....
The wild, the lobo-wild scent of the huisache blossom;
The woman touch of ceniza...
The great grass blowing.

—from *Song to Randado*
by John Houghton Allen

CONTENTS

List of Illustrations	*page* xi
Preface	xiii
Acknowledgments	xvii
Genealogy	xix
Part I: Childhood	1
Part II: Independence	65
Part III: With Pell	101
Part IV: Independence, Again	165
Bibliography	215

ILLUSTRATIONS

Helen, two or three years old *following page* 4
Ike Sewell and son Harold
House at Tipperary farm
Mattie feeding turkeys
Ike with cow and calf

Helen in riding habit,
    c. 1914 *following page* 68
Garland in riding habit, c. 1914
Mrs. Ralph McCampbell
Helen, Alleene, and Garland in pila
Helen, Garland, and Alleene at Santa Rita
Helen with two calves
Helen and Johnny Lipps
Helen, summer 1916
Helen in model-T Ford
Helen in graduation dress
Helen and Miss Pentecost in front of new
    school
Mrs. Jack Miles, Howard, Mary Hoffman,
    and Helen with deer
Texas Ranger P. B. Harbison

Helen and Pell in serapes
    and sombreros *following page* 104
Helen and Pell on sand dune
Pell and Helen, shortly after marriage
Pell and Helen on steps of Helen's house
Mattie and Ike Sewell
Hazel with hand in fishbowl

Illustrations

Pell and Helen's ranch house
Reginald spreading chopped cane in silo

Four Sewell sisters, c. 1960   *following page* 168
Helen with grandchildren, c. 1965
Helen, c. 1975
Helen and flowers

MAP

Jim Hogg County   *page* xiv

PREFACE

Sometime in the spring of 1984 Lloyd Lyman of the Texas A&M University Press told me he had heard of an eighty-eight-year-old lady who had for many years been operating a ranch in the brush country of South Texas. He thought there might be a story there that would fit into the A&M Press series about Texas lifestyles, and he wondered whether I might be interested in checking it out. So I took my tape recorder and headed for a spot on the semi-desert prairie, about fifty miles east of Laredo and about the same distance north of the Rio Grande.

I found Helen Sewell Harbison on her ranch, a few miles south of the small town of Hebbronville, and it didn't take long to realize that the lady I had found was extraordinary. She had lived through many experiences of the kind of which novels are made. She was indeed eighty-eight years old. And until she retired a few months before my visit she had been operating her ranch alone, with only the help of hired hands, for nearly thirty years. Her mind was clear, her memories were vivid, and she was unusually articulate.

During the next year and a half I made frequent trips to the Harbison ranch, for long sessions of interviews that I recorded.

Mrs. Harbison and I had an understanding: that I would not preserve the tapes; that she would read the manuscript before it went to the publisher; and that I would not publish anything against her will. The story of her life, entwined with the story of Hebbronville and Jim Hogg County, rolled onto the tape in a delightful, uninhibited fashion. She made no attempt to direct the interviews or the writing of the book, but sometimes she would tell me a delicious tidbit and then her eyes would sparkle and she'd say, "Now, I don't want that in the book!" Needless to say, her wishes have been respected.

The recording sessions were only part of my experience with Helen Harbison. When I was at the ranch I accompanied her everyplace she

Preface

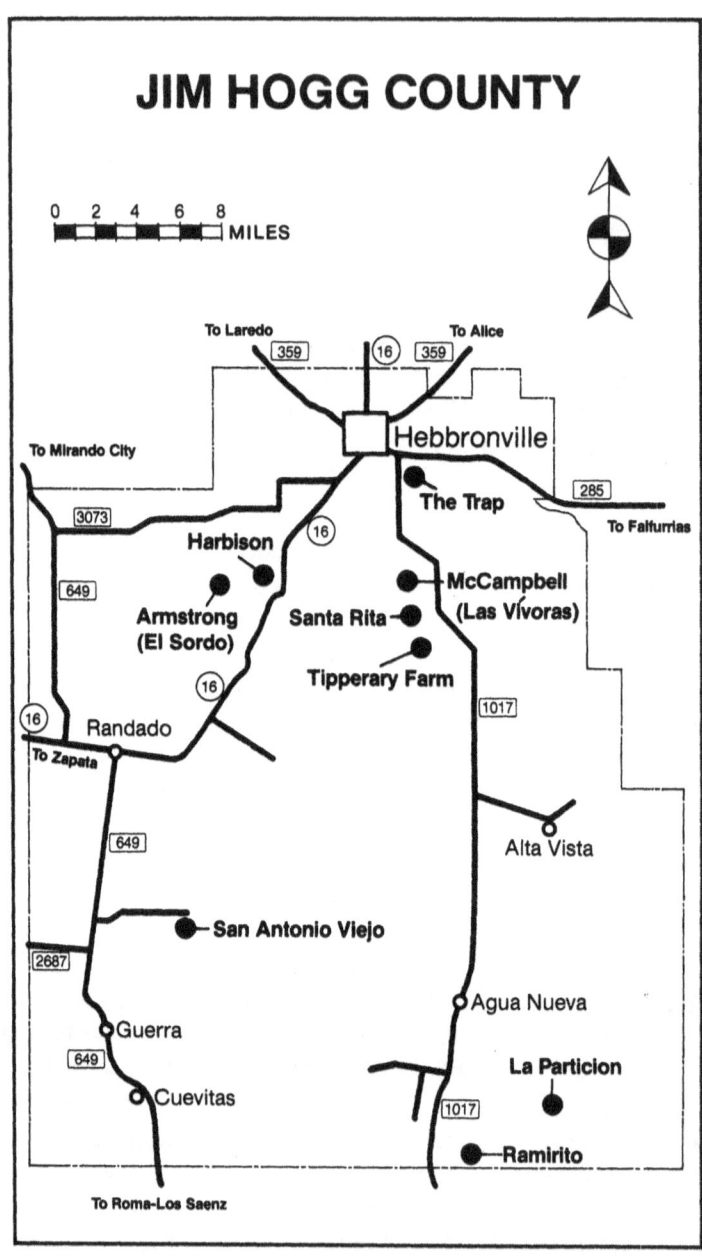

Jim Hogg County, after a map Helen made of Hebbronville area, showing locations of the different ranches mentioned in the story. Drawn by William Colville.

PREFACE

went: we attended services at the Methodist Church in Hebbronville; we did research at the library and the courthouse; we grocery shopped, went out to lunch, attended funerals, called on friends, and went to club meetings and parties on other ranches in the area.

I gathered the material for this book from various sources. Besides the interviews with Mrs. Harbison, I conducted several hours of interviews with each of her five living children (Hazel, Georgia, Reginald, Alice, and Ida), with one of her grandchildren (Cynthia Harlan), with one of her sons-in-law (Hazel's husband, Paul Roehr), and with her only remaining sibling (her brother Howard). Also, Mrs. Harbison made available to me copies of the letters she had written to her married children over a period of almost forty years, and her personal notebooks in which she had recorded genealogical information and memoirs.

In addition, I maintained close touch with Mrs. Harbison and all of her children through telephone calls and letters. Reginald, her only son, who is trained in geology, geophysics, and oceanography, and who through experience is knowledgeable about all aspects of ranching in that area, provided details for the chapter that shows the relationship of the geology to the structural stability of the ranch house, and for those chapters that deal with the mechanics of the operation of the ranch.

All of Mrs. Harbison's daughters helped with the spelling of names, and with anything else having to do with accuracy. Especially, Ida Harbison Luttrell, a writer of children's books who lives in Houston, wrote many letters and met with me numerous times to help catch errors, clear up ambiguities and misconceptions, and offer suggestions.

Unfortunately, Mrs. Harbison died of a heart attack in November of 1985. By that time I had finished gathering material for the book and had written the first fourteen chapters, which she read and approved. In solving problems that came up after her death, I continued to have assistance from her children—who read and approved the final draft of the manuscript—and from other knowledgeable people in the Hebbronville area.

In order to substantiate what Mrs. Harbison told me, I consulted respected books and periodicals, government reports, official maps, abstracts of deeds, and authorities in such fields as botany and water-well drilling.

In this book, the names of people and places are real. I have tried to be sure that the dates are correct. I believe the incidents are true.

ACKNOWLEDGMENTS

In my research for this book I have had gracious assistance from many people. I am particularly indebted to Helen Sewell Harbison's children—Reginald Harbison, Hazel Roehr, Georgia Harlan, Alice Hempel, and Ida Luttrell—for help in my search for information, for numerous readings of the manuscript, and for cooperation in every possible way. Mrs. Harbison's brother, Howard Sewell, supplied interesting detail of life at the Sewell farm during the years he and Helen were growing up, and he was especially helpful in assisting me with the collection of specimens of the plants and shrubs of Jim Hogg County.

I am indebted to Marcus Mason, retired teacher and school administrator of Houston County, and to Jo Anne Daily, retired teacher, Grapeland, for information about the operation of secondary schools in Texas during the first half of the twentieth century; to Mrs. Sam Hill Newman of Grapeland, Mrs. Deloris J. Duff of Eli Lilly and Company, and Dr. Albert R. Machel and Ava Bush, both retired from teaching at Stephen F. Austin University, for help with research on nux vomica and other poisons; to Dr. Elenor R. Cox and Dr. Clarissa Kimber of Texas A&M University, for help in identifying specimens of South Texas botany; to James Waldrop, Crockett, Dr. James Robinson, entomologist, Overton, and Dr. H. R. Burke, Department of Entomology, Texas A&M University, for assistance in researching the history of the boll weevil; to Dillard Wied of Hebbronville for information about waterwell drilling in Jim Hogg County; to Ernest Haner, Hebbronville, for help with the map of Jim Hogg County; and to Edna Glendenning, also of Hebbronville, for the loan of out-of-print books about that area; also to James Gibbs, Glenn Cross, Saundra Stowe, Bertha Roberts, and Dorothy English, all of Crockett, for assistance in running down important bits of information.

Pamela Palmer, Don Richter, and Betty Bennett, librarians at Ste-

Acknowledgments

phen F. Austin University Library; Mary Wright at San Antonio Public Library; Judy Zipp, librarian, and Fane Burt, editorial writer, at the San Antonio *Express and News;* Douglas Weiskopf and his staff at Houston Public Library; Betty J. Newman at the Jim Hogg County Public Library; and Sallie Woodward and Betty Kendrick and their staff at the Crockett Public Library—all have been patient and helpful.

My friends Lulu S. Brand, William N. Barnard, Sr., Dorothy Mills, J. W. and Viola Arnett, Clarence and Rebecca Kennedy, Earnest and Edith Armstrong, Robert and Mae Wickboldt, and Wyncie Dell Barnhill all gave unstintingly of their time to help me in any way they could.

I acknowledge my great debt to Frank and Rosemary Wardlaw for critical reading of the manuscript and for helpful suggestions and continuous encouragement.

And to my own caring family I am indebted for helpful suggestions, critical readings of the manuscript, and hearty encouragement and support.

GENEALOGY

Isaac Newton Sewell — married Martha Bell Linville

  Emil
  Alleene
  Opal
  Helen Marie — married Pelton Bruce Harbison
  Garland
  Harold
  Howard

    Hazel Maurine — married Paul Roehr
        Daphne
        Paul Bruce

    Georgia Isabel — married Vernon Harlan
        Cynthia
        Martin

    Reginald Newton — married Beverly Blanchard

    Donia Ione (died in infancy)

    Alice Louise — married Lou Hempel
        Alice Louise

    Ida Alleene — married William Luttrell
        Robert
        Anne
        William
        Richard

    Carrie Lee — married Robert Anderson
        Robert Clyde
        Jennifer
        Meredith
        (Alice Louise)

Childhood

CHAPTER ONE

It was February, 1908, and in the little town of Osawatomie, Kansas, last night's rain had changed to snow, which by afternoon was beginning to be driven by a brisk wind. Eleven-year-old Helen Sewell looked out the window now and then as she stuffed her few belongings into the old trunk that already held clothes and other possessions of her brothers and sisters.

Mattie Sewell, Helen's mother, had packed for her three sons: one-year-old Howard and six-year-old Harold were too young to do their packing, and nineteen-year-old Emil could not be depended upon to do his. But Mattie expected her daughters to do their own. Thirteen-year-old Opal, mature and reliable, had done hers early. Nine-year-old Garland's clothes were on top, all neatly and precisely folded. Helen's were the last to be packed. She did it casually, her mind on other things.

Well, it was really going to happen. Tomorrow they were going to Texas. Helen wasn't exactly sure how she felt about it. She couldn't help being excited about the train trip. And her father had said the new farm was better than any place they had ever lived. But she had to fight back the tears every time she thought of leaving Marguerite, her very, very best ever friend. When would they see each other again? And there was Kyle. He had picked her out from all those pretty girls at the party and had asked if he could walk home with her. She—with those awful freckles all over her face. Never mind that he had brought his little brother along because he would be afraid to walk back home alone in the dark. Or that her mother had sent Opal to put a stop to her "date": "Mama says for you to get home right this minute!" Never mind all of that. Kyle *had* wanted to walk her home. It still made her feel kind of giddy every time she thought about it. And he had slipped a post card to her at recess yesterday. It was the kind of card hotels give out to people who stay there. Kyle's father worked for the railroad; he'd probably picked it up someplace when he was away on busi-

Childhood

ness. It was a picture of a hotel lobby. On the back it said: "To Helen from Kyle." That was all. She examined it carefully once more before she tucked it among her things in the trunk. Her mother might be angry if she saw it. Helen remembered that her big sister Alleene had been spanked for going to a party in clothes her parents disapproved of one time when she came home for a visit from Kansas State Normal School. A person needed to be a little careful about parents.

Her mind turned to Alleene. She was the only one of the family who was not going to Texas. She was to stay with an aunt in Emporia in order to finish her education and get a teacher's certificate. It must be fun to be seventeen, and be going to college, and have lots of pretty clothes. Helen looked at her own best dress as she carelessly folded it into the trunk. It was a hand-me-down from Opal. Well, most all of Helen's clothes were hand-me-downs. She became angry all over again as she remembered the lovely dresses her Aunt Ethel had willed to her, but that her mother had made over for Alleene. Aunt Ethel had such beautiful dresses, and Helen had always loved to open the closet door and just look at them, to rub her hands over them. She had asked her aunt once, "If you ever die, can I have your clothes?"

Ethel had laughed. "Well, I don't expect to die any time soon. But if I do, I'll will you my clothes." And when, a year later, she came down with a terminal illness she remembered her promise and asked her husband to give her clothes to Helen.

The clothes had been duly delivered to the Sewell house. But Helen had not gotten even one dress of them. Her mother had explained, "Alleene needs them, and they're too old for you, anyway."

Helen was still bitter about it. She jammed Opal's hand-me-down into the trunk.

"Oh, Helen. . . . Will you come here?" Mattie Sewell called from the kitchen.

"Yes, Mama." Helen banged the trunk lid down, glanced again at the snow the wind was whipping around the corner of the house, and went to learn what her mother wanted.

In the kitchen was a neighbor who had brought a pot of soup for their supper. Mattie told Helen: "You know that gas hotplate that's there on the back porch? Well, Mrs. Smith here says that new woman that moved into the old Wilcox house across the railroad tracks was looking for one of them. I want you to run over there with it and see if she'll buy it. You'll have to pull it like a sled, it's too heavy for you

CHAPTER ONE

Helen (two or three years old) with rose in hand.

Childhood

Ike Sewell and his son Harold, on a load of cotton, in Hebbronville. *Below:* Back view of the house at Tipperary Farm, showing the boarded-up back porch. This was taken after Helen and Garland were married. The people in the photo are Garland and her son Leuin David, Jr.

CHAPTER ONE

Mattie feeding her turkeys at Tipperary Farm. *Below:* Ike, with cow and calf, at Tipperary Farm.

Childhood

to carry. Tell her I want two dollars for it. Bundle up good, now. Looks like it's getting cold out there." She turned to Mrs. Smith. "Two dollars is two dollars."

Mrs. Smith looked at Helen's feet and said, "Put your galoshes on."

"She don't have any galoshes," Mattie said.

"My goodness!" said Mrs. Smith. "I wouldn't let one of mine out of the house on a day like this without galoshes."

"Well, you've just got two to buy for," Mattie told her. "We've got seven. None of ours got galoshes."

Helen tied a rope to the hotplate and started off in a run, dragging it over the ice and snow, keeping her head down to shield her face from the blowing snow. Once, she almost bumped into a man who was delivering groceries. He told her: "Little girl, you better get home. This snow's turning into a blizzard. You're liable to freeze."

But Helen had no thought of turning back before her mission was accomplished. She plunged on through the snow. When she arrived at her destination she learned that the lady had already bought a hotplate, that morning. She turned around and started dragging her burden back home—going more slowly now because her feet were so numb she could no longer run on them. When she stumbled into the kitchen she began to cry. She told her mother, "My feet feel like chunks of wood."

Mattie said, "Land a goshen, child! If I'd realized it was that cold out there I'd never a-sent you." She heated a pan of water and told Helen to put her feet in it. Helen cried harder, because the hot water made her feet hurt. Her face and hands were numb, and they began to hurt also as the air of the kitchen warmed them. "Gracious!" said Mattie to Mrs. Smith. "And then she didn't *buy* it."

Helen kept dipping her feet into the water, crying out each time they went in. The two women tried to ignore her. "I never thought Isaac Sewell would sell his interest in the grocery and dry goods store and go back to farming," said Mrs. Smith. "Do you think you're really gonna like that place in Texas, Mattie? I mean, with it being away off out in the country like that?"

"That store's not doing so good," Mattie told her. "Too many bills they can't collect. Ike says he's lucky to get out of it. And he thinks this place in Texas is paradise. Well, it does *sound* like it. You know, he got us a two-story house built while he was down there this last time. He says one of the other families that bought land there has built a house, too. In fact, they're the ones that's gonna meet the children

CHAPTER ONE

and me at the train, and we're gonna stay with them till Ike gets down there with the furniture and farm things, and the animals."

"I thought a lot of families bought land there," said Mrs. Smith.

"Well, yes, they did," Mattie said. "But the rest of them's living in tents. Just been two houses built so far—ours and the Danhausers'."

Mrs. Smith walked over to the window and looked out. "Must be plenty different from here, if people can live in tents this time of year."

"Oh, yes," said Mattie. "It is. Ike's already broke us a garden plot. He borrowed some mules and a plow and done it before he came home. He says we can grow things the year round, so I won't have to can all those vegetables every summer. And he's getting us a well drilled. He's already bought a windmill to go on it. They pump their water with windmills in Texas. Everybody's got one."

"Well, sounds like he has you pretty well set up down there."

"Yes," said Mattie. "And he says they grow a lot of orange trees. Imagine being able to go out and pick oranges off your own tree! And Bermuda onions. They grow fields of Bermuda onions. Ike thinks he's gonna get rich growing onions. Them onions *are expensive* to buy in the stores."

"I thought maybe you wanted to get away from here on account of Emil," Mrs. Smith said.

"Now why would I want to do that?" demanded Mattie, angrily. "Emil's doing better. He's just fine."

Mrs. Smith changed the subject. Helen knew her mother was simply defending Emil, as she always did. She knew Emil was one of the reasons they were moving; she'd heard her parents talking.

Emil was their oldest child. He was going to be twenty years old in a couple of months, and he was not right. Not right in his body. And beginning to be not right in his mind.

He had been one of the brightest boys in his high school class. Then, when he and some other boys were fooling around with gunpowder one Fourth of July, some powder had blown up in Emil's face, and he had not been the same since. About a year ago he had jumped off a high cliff and damaged his spine and now he was very crippled. And recently he had been getting harder and harder for his parents to control. Helen heard Mattie tell Ike she thought Emil would get well in his mind if they could get him away from people "that treat him like he's crazy." And Helen believed that was why Mattie was so willing to pick up and move away off down there in Texas.

Childhood

But Helen didn't think that was the main reason Ike wanted to go to Texas. She had heard the man from Fowler and Rankin Real Estate Company talking about how wonderful it was at this place where his company was selling land, and she noticed how her father's eyes shone as he listened.

She had often heard her mother say, "That freckled-faced Ike Sewell's a dreamer." And once she heard Mattie telling Aunt Ethel, "Every time we've moved Ike's been sure we was getting into something better, but it's not always been that way." Helen suspected that if Emil had been well Mattie might not have been so willing to go to Texas.

The next morning, in the midst of a blizzard, Mattie and her children boarded the train for their new home. Alleene, of course, was not with them; she was in Emporia going to college. Ike was not with them, either. He would come on the freight train, along with their furniture, a wagon and some plows and cultivators, a team of draft horses, and Mattie's chickens. It was necessary that he ride the freight train so he could care for the horses and chickens during the trip. He had to buy the horses in Kansas because he found no draft horses for sale in South Texas. Everybody down there used mules for that kind of work. Ike thought he had to have horses. He had grown up on farms in Ohio and Missouri, and he had farmed off and on after he and Mattie married. He had always used horses; he had never worked mules.

Mattie and the children rode the day coach for four days and three nights. If there was a dining car Helen never saw it—Mattie packed enough food to last all that time. Helen and Garland amused themselves by calling out the names of things they could see from the train window. And by the time they got into the southern part of Texas what they could see was new and different. They looked out on sandy, semi-desert low rolling prairies that were sparsely covered with mesquite, prickly pear cactus, and a strange plant the train conductor said was called yucca. After that, every time they saw one of those plants Helen would call out "Yucca!" and Garland would say "Yacca!" It was *yucca, yacca, yucca, yacca* all day—two blithe spirits coping with life.

At Laredo they changed to the little narrow-gauge Tex-Mex train that made one trip each day between Laredo and Corpus Christi. It was still *yucca, yacca, yucca, yacca*.

About fifty miles east of Laredo they got off at a place called Hebbronville, where they saw a few dusty, one-story, wooden structures, the most noticeable of which was the prominently marked office of

CHAPTER ONE

Fowler and Rankin Real Estate Company. The sun was shining. It was nice and warm. In fact, it was hot. The depot was surrounded by open fields that were covered with many kinds of wildflowers. While Mattie and Opal helped Mr. Danhauser load their things onto his wagon, Helen and Garland ran wild, gathering armfuls of flowers, rejoicing in the sunshine. And during the long fifteen-mile ride from the depot to the Danhauser home, the two little girls often jumped from the wagon to gather more wildflowers, or just to run along barefoot in the soft warm sand. When they were tired they could easily climb back on the wagon because the mules moved slowly as they pulled the loaded wagon through the deep sand.

When they were about halfway home, the cold weather they had left in Kansas caught up with them in the form of a Texas "norther," and Mattie had to get out her quilts to wrap everybody in, because the temperature dropped many degrees in a few minutes. They arrived at the Danhauser house feeling almost as uncomfortable as when they left Kansas in the blizzard. It was their first lesson in Texas weather.

The morning after their arrival, Mattie and her children walked the mile from the Danhauser house to their own new home. Mattie looked at the plowed garden plot and said, "Just look at that red dirt! I'll bet it's old hard clay." She climbed through the barbed wire fence Ike had built. When she felt of the soil her expression changed. "Oh, my! It's so mellow!" she beamed.

Some men were there at the Sewell place that day, setting up equipment, getting ready to drill the water well and install the windmill.

In the early days in South Texas, water wells were dug by hand, and mules were used to haul the displaced earth to the surface in pouches made of cowhide. After a well was producing, mules were used again, to lift cowhide "buckets" of water.

But by the time the Sewells arrived in Texas in 1908 wells were being drilled by cable tool rigs that were powered by portable wood-burning steam engines. This equipment was mounted on wide metal wheels and was pulled by mules from one drilling site to the next. Barrels of water used in the drilling process were brought to the site by wagon and mule team. And the men who did the drilling set up camp and lived there while they were drilling a well. Water from these wells was pumped by windmills and stored in wooden or galvanized tanks, or in ponds called "pilas," which were much like the water-storage ponds that in East Texas are called "dirt tanks."

Childhood

Helen and the others watched, fascinated, as the men prepared to create for them what in this place it was not possible to live without — a dependable water supply. And that evening Helen talked her mother out of a precious postage stamp so she could write to her friend Marguerite and tell her about their adventures in Texas. Neither Helen nor her mother knew then how difficult it would turn out to be to get that letter mailed.

When Ike arrived they moved into their new house.

The first dwellings in the area around Hebbronville had been constructed of stone, but after the Tex-Mex Railroad was built in the late 1870s a few people began to ship in lumber that they used for building simple wooden structures. Later, a few pretentious homes of wood construction were built in town and on some of the big ranches, but when the Sewells arrived — and for several years afterward — Hebbronville consisted mostly of dusty shacks scattered over the prairie.

Ike bought the lumber for his house from Edds and Acklen Lumber Company. It had been shipped to Hebbronville by train and was transported the fifteen miles out to the farm by wagon and mule team. The outside walls of the house consisted of vertical one-by-twelve-inch rough boards, with one-by-two-inch boards covering the cracks. The house was not sealed on the inside. The windows were glass — unscreened. The doors were unscreened. The downstairs was one large room and a kitchen. Mattie and Ike used the large room for a bedroom, and the whole family used it for a sitting room. The children all slept in the unpartitioned upstairs. They hung a piece of canvas to divide it into two rooms: one for the boys and one for the girls.

Mattie had moved her prize possession — a Home Comfort cooking range that had a warming oven and a ten-gallon hot-water reservoir — and she persuaded Ike to install it in the new kitchen, even before the beds were set up. She also brought some handmade carpet that she laid on the floor of the downstairs sitting-sleeping room, and at the end of the day, after the furniture was all unpacked and the house was in order, she surveyed the room and remarked, "Carpet sure helps to make a house look like a home."

The yard around the new Sewell house was littered with pieces of lumber, some with nails sticking up in them. Mattie ordered her children not to go out of the house without their shoes. Helen, however, not in a mood to be restrained, went out to walk barefoot in the sand. She found a big pile of ashes near the new well and walked cautiously

CHAPTER ONE

into the edge of it. The ashes felt even softer than the sand. How wonderful! She plowed in and was in the middle of the pile when she realized there were live coals under there. Before she could get out her feet were badly burned, sending her into uncontrollable screams.

Mattie got her into the house and brought kerosene in a blue enameled cup, thinking to bathe the burned feet in that. Helen, in her distress, thought the cup contained water and she grabbed it and took a big gulp before Mattie could stop her. Now the problems were multiplied—for mother and child, too. Helen stopped screaming and turned pale. Mattie wrapped the corner of her apron around her finger and ran it down Helen's throat. When she could stop vomiting, Helen started to scream again. Ike came to find out what was going on, and Mattie screamed at him, "What did I ever do to deserve this child!"

Helen knew that over the years she had often been a source of worry to her mother. For instance, one time after the Barnum and Bailey Circus had been in town Helen, wishing to be a circus performer but having no proper attire, stripped down to her union suit and went out in the yard and climbed on a box and started kicking up her heels. This went on at the exact time the Methodist minister was walking down the sidewalk past the Sewell home, and Helen's mother was emerging from a neighbor's house across the street. After the minister stared for a while he was heard to mutter, "What kind of parent would allow that?"

And then there was the time Helen caused Harold to break his leg. He was two or three at the time. She had persuaded him to climb into a little pony cart that was kept in the barnyard, and she was pulling him around. When he wanted to get out she refused to stop. Helen was having fun, but Harold apparently wasn't. He climbed over the side and got his leg caught in the wheel. He began to scream. Then Helen began to scream. Mattie came running. When Helen saw Harold's leg dangling at a strange angle she went and hid behind the barn. Nobody paid any attention to her; they were all busy taking care of Harold. But she kept watching the house, and when she saw the doctor arrive she sneaked back and looked in the window and watched him set Harold's leg. Well. Those were but two of the many times. Helen knew that. She didn't really mean to be a problem. Alleene said she was impetuous—whatever that meant.

As it turned out, Helen's feet were so badly burned that she could not walk for six weeks. Mattie doctored her with poultices of grated

Childhood

raw Irish potatoes, a remedy recommended by the big doctor book (*Medicology, or Home Encyclopedia of Health, A Complete Family Guide*, by Joseph G. Richardson et al.) she had brought with her from Kansas.

In the early 1900s many people all over the country turned to a doctor only when someone in the family was critically ill. Mattie's doctor book was probably already well used even before they moved to Texas. But now it was a lifesaver. There was no way to get to a doctor. There was not even a doctor in Hebbronville then, nor for a good many years to come.

CHAPTER TWO

The land Ike and the other northerners bought in 1908 was not fenced when they bought it. It had never been fenced, though barbed wire was being used in South Texas by the late 1870s. This was isolated land, in the middle of an area between the Nueces River and the Rio Grande that was known as the Nueces Strip, an area that had been a no-man's land—where a sheriff seldom lived out his term—from the time of the Texas War for Independence until well after the Civil War. It was open-range grasslands and, though it was not public land, South Texas cattle barons in 1908 treated it as if it were. They grazed their herds there at will.

Most of the area consisted of big grants—chunks of many thousands of acres each—that had been made to individuals before Texas won its independence from Mexico. Prior to 1821 the grants had been made by the king of Spain, but after Mexico became independent the governors of some of its provinces made grants also. Almost all of the grantees were Spanish. Many of them had established substantial, though isolated, habitations on their grants, and had lived there until the Texas revolution came along.

After Sam Houston whipped Santa Ana at the battle of San Jacinto, both Mexico and the Republic of Texas claimed sovereignty over the land between the Nueces and the Rio Grande but neither paid much attention to it. Renegades from both sides of the border drifted into the sparsely settled area and tried to survive by any means necessary. There was practically no law and order. And, although the Republic of Texas recognized and honored the Spanish and Mexican grants and land titles, many of the old Spanish families fled. Land in South Texas became cheap. "Anglos" with plenty of guts and a little money moved in and established large ranches.

Although few of the fleeing Spanish ranchers came back, two members of one family returned to the Hebbronville area. Captain José María

Childhood

Benavides and his brother Don Ignacio Benavides came in 1868 to claim the large Noriecitas grant that in 1740 had been given by the king of Spain to their ancestor, Simón de Hinojosa. Descendants of the family still live on and work the Noriecitas ranch south of Hebbronville. Hebbronville itself is located on part of the Noriecitas grant.

And fifteen miles south of Hebbronville, descendants of Don Hipolito Garcia still live at Randado, the village that grew up around the headquarters of his 80,000-acre Randado ranch, where in the early days men driving oxen and the archaic two-wheeled carts came from Mexico to trade. This is the village John Houghton Allen celebrated in his *Song to Randado*.

But the land Isaac Sewell bought had never been part of a Spanish grant—it apparently had remained ungranted. Twelve sections of land —7,680 acres in all—that joined the San Antonio de Baluarte grant on the north and the Palitos Blancos grant on the west were given by the State of Texas to the Central and Montgomery Railroad Company, and eventually these sections ended up in the hands of the enterprising Fowler and Rankin Real Estate people, who persuaded Ike and other Kansans to buy small tracts.

Selling South Texas land to naive northerners through exaggeration and half-truths was big business around the turn of the century. Real estate companies engaged in this type of venture maintained offices in prominent cities across the country, advertised in newspapers, distributed brochures—always touting the merits of their particular lands of paradise. They used essentially identical techniques: each prepared and maintained a showplace where trained personnel and an adequate water supply turned the semi-desert into a lush oasis and where prospective buyers were entertained and subjected to the hard sell; each arranged with the railroads to provide excursion trains with reduced rates; each met the trains with horse-drawn surreys or buggies and plied their passengers with whiskey so they would not notice how far it was from the depot to the land that was for sale.

Fowler and Rankin's showplace was called Santa Rita. Here a professional horticulturist by the name of Will Sponsellor grew many kinds of vegetables the year around and displayed healthy groves of lemon and orange trees and a vineyard containing numerous varieties of grapes, all watered by an artesian well. And here Fowler and Rankin's salesmen took prospects to feast their eyes and their appetites on the abundance of this incomparable land.

CHAPTER TWO

Santa Rita was a beautiful place. It is easy to see how men already feeling rosy from all that free liquor fell under its charm. It was maybe two or three miles from what became the Sewell farm.

The northerners had to build fences to keep out the range cattle that were accustomed to run free over this land. Ike worked at fencing his farm while the carpenters built his house, so when he moved his family to Texas he was ready to start breaking his land. He hitched his two horses — Nellie and Charlie — to his big plow and he himself rode it, plowing two rows at a time. He bought an old mule named Sam and hitched him to the one-row middle buster and put Opal to work walking behind that.

After Helen's feet healed, she also worked in the field. She walked behind the mule and the single-row plow half of each day, while Opal worked at the house doing the laundry, washing dishes, sweeping out tracked-in sand. Then Opal worked in the field the other half of the day while Helen worked around the house.

Helen didn't like housework. She hated standing over an ironing board with a flatiron that she had to keep a fire going in the cookstove to heat. And she never could get the floor swept clear of sand. That sand was everywhere, especially in Mattie's beloved handmade carpet. There just wasn't any way to get it out. But Helen liked field work, and she enjoyed working with her father. She didn't mind the hard physical labor. She developed a strong body and the strong arms necessary to control a hard-mouthed mule.

The plows could be converted to planters by changing attachments. Ike and the girls continued to work in the fields. They planted corn, a crop Ike knew well. And they planted cane and cotton, two crops he had never planted before. The cane was for feeding the horses and mule, the corn was for feeding the family as well as the animals, and the cotton was a money crop. In theory it seemed sound. Ike had hoped to plant Bermuda onions, but they didn't get it done that year.

Everybody worked except the two little boys, and of course Emil. Mattie planted and tended a garden and did all of the cooking. She was an excellent cook. She could turn out a nourishing and appetizing meal from whatever materials were at hand. She knew how to "make do." Garland was not considered strong enough to work in the field, but she helped with the garden and the housework, doing everything carefully and well. Nobody expected Emil to do any work. He sat in a rocking chair on the front porch most of the day, reading Mattie's doctor book. Harold and Howard played; they were too little to work.

One evening Helen and Ike came in from the field to find Mattie and Opal on their hands and knees, pulling the tacks that held the carpet to the floor. Mattie looked up at them with a sweat- and dirt-streaked face and said, "The sand is cutting it to pieces." Nobody else said anything. Mattie and Opal went on with their tack pulling. Ike turned and went out the back door. Helen followed. She knew where to find him. He kept an old chair by the north side of the house, the only place where there was any shade, and when he felt discouraged he would sit there and puff on his corncob pipe. She seated herself on the ground beside his chair, and the two of them sat there without talking until Mattie called them to supper.

Mattie had been gradually cleaning up the yard, using the scrap lumber to fuel her cookstove. When she neared the end of that and told Ike she was about out of firewood, she was shocked to learn that he would have to go for miles to get wood from a small grove of mesquite, where he had gotten the posts he used in building his fences. She had seen plenty of mesquite from the train window when they came across Texas, but it was true that there was only a small shrub here and there on their property. It would be a couple of decades before mesquite brush and prickly pear cactus moved in and covered this land.

The Sewell family settled more or less happily into its new situation, in spite of such disappointments as the scarcity of wood for the cookstove and the lack of a carpet on the sitting-room floor. Nobody seemed to be overly concerned that there was no doctor, no church, no school within reach.

They gradually became acquainted with their neighbors. Besides the Danhausers, they met the Meades and Huffs and a few other families who lived in tents. And they met the Sponsellors who lived at Santa Rita. They also met Neville Hinnant, a cowboy who lived at Santa Rita and was in charge of some range cattle that grazed in that area, cattle that belonged to the wealthy rancher W. W. Jones.

Neville rode to the Sewell place one Sunday afternoon with a big grin on his face, waving a letter in his hand. The letter was for Helen — from her friend Marguerite. He said it had been lying around at Santa Rita for a couple of weeks and he decided to bring it over and get acquainted. Helen was so excited she could hardly get the letter opened. She ran out behind the house to read it.

Sundays at the farm were not much different from other days. The

CHAPTER TWO

Sewells got up at the same early hour, ate at the same regular times, did the chores around the house. There was one thing that was different, however—they did not work in the fields on Sundays, because Mattie thought that was a sin. Mattie took her religion seriously. Before she and Ike married he had loved to go to baseball games on Sunday afternoons, but Mattie put a stop to that. So, even if there had been Sunday baseball games that Ike could have attended in South Texas, he would not have been able to go because Mattie would not have tolerated it.

Marguerite's letter said there was still snow and ice in Kansas. She thought Texas sounded wonderful and wished she were there. She said Kyle and his family had moved from Osawatomie—Marguerite didn't know where to. There was a new girl in their class at school. The boys liked her. The girls didn't. She wondered why Helen didn't mail her letter to Marguerite when she first wrote it—it was postmarked in Hebbronville exactly one month after the date at the top of the letter. Helen was beginning to learn about mail service in Texas.

Of course there was no mail delivery to the few isolated farms out fifteen miles over a sandy trail from the little post office in the general store in Hebbronville. But anybody going or coming between Santa Rita and Hebbronville would carry outgoing and incoming mail, as a courtesy to the neighbors. Sometimes it was a while between trips.

At first things at the Sewell farm went well. The sandy loam was easy to work, and winter rains had left enough moisture to sprout the seeds. Mattie's hens began to lay, and some of them wanted to set. She sent away for turkey and guinea eggs and hatched them under the chicken hens.

Mattie had moved canned fruit and vegetables from Kansas. Ike ordered canned sardines and salmon by the crate, and green coffee beans by the hundred pounds, from a wholesale place in Laredo. They suffered no shortage of food those first months in Texas.

By April the days were hot, the sun beat down, the arid wind blew, and rainfall was almost nil. Mattie's garden began to wilt during the day, and she started carrying water to it in buckets. She didn't know it then, but this would be a pattern she would follow for many years in order to feed her family.

The riding and walking plows were changed from planters to cultivators, and the field work went on. They had to thin the cotton. It was a big job, and the whole family—except the two little boys and Emil—worked at it. The accepted way to thin cotton was by chopping

Childhood

it with a hoe. But they didn't have enough hoes to go around, so Helen learned to thin it by catching a little cotton plant between her toes and pulling it out of the ground.

Another important thing Mattie moved from Kansas was her Singer sewing machine, and with its help she now made everything she and her children wore, even their underclothes. For the girls she made loose-fitting cotton dresses that they wore in the field as well as around the house. They didn't need any dress-up clothes — they never went anyplace. She got Ike to order the fabric from Sears, Roebuck and Company. He selected it himself. Mattie believed he knew more about it than she did because of his experience in his grocery and dry goods store.

He ordered shoes for the family. Mattie never went shopping. She never even went to Hebbronville — the long trip in a wagon over those sandy trails did not appeal to her. She simply told Ike what she needed and expected him to get it. In fact, Ike had always done the buying for the family, even before they moved to Texas. He had caused Helen great disappointment once when he took her and Garland to buy Easter hats and vetoed Helen's choice of a lacy red hat trimmed in flowers, buying for them instead two almost identical sailors with grosgrain streamers.

When the Sewells first lived in Texas herds of antelope roamed the area around Santa Rita, and they often played near the Sewells' yard, or in their fields. They played like goats, jumping up and butting heads. Antelope are curious about anything new or different in the environment. They seemed to enjoy watching the Sewells as much as the Sewells enjoyed watching them. It was against the law to kill one. There were no deer; they didn't move in until after the brush came.

Sometimes the Sewells saw, or heard, a bobcat. They heard coyotes almost every night and frequently saw one in the daytime. The bobcats and coyotes would have liked to get Mattie's chickens and other fowl, but the Sewells had brought a little rat terrier with them from Kansas, and he put on a show of ferocity every time he smelled bobcat or coyote. He did the same when he came across a rattlesnake, but he was afraid of rattlesnakes; he never got close enough for one to strike him.

Once Mattie sent Helen under the house to look for a hen's nest. She had been hearing a hen cackling under there as if she just laid an egg. Eggs were precious. Well, everything was precious here in this isolated place. So Mattie wanted to save those egss. She told Helen:

CHAPTER TWO

"Go crawl under the house and see if you can find that nest. I know there's one under there, someplace."

Helen pushed her head and shoulders under a sill and came face to face with a big coiled rattlesnake. Fortunately, it did not strike. Rattlesnakes are usually not quick to strike unless they are attacked. This one simply rattled. Helen came out from under the house screaming.

Ike and the little dog came running from the windmill. Mattie came running from the garden, a rake in her hand. Ike was nervous. This was the first time one of the children had an encounter with a rattler. He was able to pull the snake out with the garden rake, but he didn't want to chance breaking the rake by trying to kill the snake with it. He picked up a stick but it broke the first time he hit the snake. The rattler struck the stick, apparently unhurt. The little dog was barking but it took care not to get close enough for the snake to reach it. Ike finally got a mesquite limb he had hauled in to chop up for stovewood. The limb was big, and heavy. Ike was excited, and his hands were shaking, so he was clumsy. But man finally won over snake.

After that they kept a big hoe propped against the house, and several times they had to use it to kill a rattler. One day the little dog came to the back door, barking. Mattie told him to go away and shut up. He kept going out to the garden and then coming back to bark at the door. Finally he went and got the hoe handle in his mouth and dragged the hoe to the back door and then barked. Mattie said, "Land a goshen! He's trying to tell me something!" She picked up the hoe and followed the dog. Beside the garden gate was a big rattler, coiled and ready to strike.

The little dog had sense enough not to get too close to a rattler, but he wasn't that wise about rabid coyotes. One afternoon he tangled with one in the cotton patch, and Ike had to shoot him. That was a sad time. The children cried, and Ike cried with them.

Once when Ike had been to Hebbronville for supplies he came home and said he had named their farm. From then on it would be called Tipperary. He said he had found the road back home so long and lonely that to help pass the time he began to sing, and that he kept singing, over and over again, "It's a Long, Long Way to Tipperary to the Sweetest *Girls* I Know."

The northerners were learning about the South Texas climate. Their crops came up looking healthy, but they began to wilt during the day.

Childhood

The wilting was particularly bad on days when a hot wind blew. Some plants died. Others were stunted. The weather became an obsession with most people. "Will it rain?" "When will it rain?" "Oh, God, please let it rain." It was the last thing they talked about at night and the first topic of conversation in the morning. The old grandmother who lived with the Danhausers prayed every time the family sat down to eat: "Heavenly Father, thank you for this food, and we'd thank you for some rain if you could see fit to send it." Every time Mr. Meade saw Ike in the fields, he said the exact same thing he had said the last time he saw him: "Good morning, Mr. Sewell. A nice breeze. Do you think it will rain?" It became monotonous.

Actually, life in general was becoming a little monotonous for Helen and Garland. The only contact they had had with the outside world was the letter from Marguerite, and now and then a package of used magazines from Ike's brother John — publications such as *Harper's Magazine*, *McCall's*, *Ladies' Home Journal*, *Good Housekeeping*. They contained short stories that the girls read over and over until they wore out the pages. They also contained fashion news and pictures of the latest styles. Helen and Garland pored over these and dreamed of becoming elegant ladies and going to New York.

Then, Ike subscribed to a newspaper. The girls were excited over that. It was the San Antonio *Semi-Weekly Express*. It came irregularly, several issues at a time, but still it was wonderful. It cost one dollar for twelve months. The part they liked best was a regular feature called "Cousins' Corner," where letters from young readers were published, and answered in future issues by other young readers. This provided communication with their peers, often with young people who were as isolated and lonely as they. It offered a remote type of social life.

Emil showed no interest in the newspaper. He was becoming more and more withdrawn. One night Helen and Garland sat hidden on the stairs and listened to Mattie and Ike talking about him. Ike said, "It looks to me like he's getting worse."

"No, he isn't!" said Mattie. "He's gonna be better. I just know it!"

Ike, said, "Now, Mat, I heard him fussing at you today. I'm getting afraid he might hurt you."

"Well, I don't want to put him away," said Mattie. "If that's what you're working up to."

Nobody said anything more. The girls sneaked back up to their bed. That wasn't the first time the two girls had been out of bed when

CHAPTER TWO

their parents thought they were asleep. They frequently got up and sat by the window, especially on moonlit nights, and entertained themselves by telling short stories. It was an idea that had occurred to them one time when long weeks passed without a package of magazines from Uncle John. Helen told Garland: "We don't have to wait for the stories in the magazines. We can make up our own stories."

Garland said, "How can we do that?"

"I'll show you," Helen told her, and she began to tell a story about a girl who fell in love with a handsome and wealthy young man who took her to lots of exciting places. The girls were washing dishes at the time, and they got so wrapped up in the story they forgot to work. Mattie came to learn what was keeping them so long, and that put a stop to the story telling. But the girls' imaginations had been unleashed. Every time they could snatch a few minutes, they'd begin telling their story again. And when it ended, they started another one. They didn't get up and sit by the window *every* night—some nights, they were so tired they went right to sleep and slept all night long. Actually, the nights were not all that long. Ike, like most farmers, got his family up for breakfast around four o'clock, so they could get out to the field by daylight.

On one of Ike's infrequent trips to town a stray dog took up with him. It followed him all day, wherever he went. Nobody seemed to know the dog, or where it came from. When Ike started home it followed his wagon. After a while he took it in beside him, and they rode home together. It was a bulldog. They named him Ben. And it wasn't long before all of them loved him.

Every time Mattie stepped out of the house Ben was right at her heels. When she was in her garden, Ben was there. One day he found a big rattlesnake in the row where she was picking beans, and he shook the snake to pieces. Mattie was sure the dog had saved her life.

But the rattler had managed to get a lick in on Ben before he finished it off. It bit him on the nose. Mattie doctored him with kerosene, and the dark green venom ran out. But Ben's head swelled to twice its normal size. He went to the place where the overflow ran from the trough at the well and stuck his head in the mud. They thought he would die. But after a few days the swelling began to go down. Ben got well, and now the family loved him more than ever.

Ben killed many rattlesnakes after that, and he finally became immune to their venom.

CHAPTER THREE

The Sewells' first year in Texas was what Neville Hinnant called "drowthy." There was practically no rain. The hot winds blew. Sometimes the sky was red with blowing sand. It got in their eyes and in their ears, and in their mouths, in their food, in their beds. Neville said, "Some years it's like this."

The merciless sun, the lack of rain, and the blowing sand made life disagreeable for people and animals, but they made it almost intolerable for plants in the field. Mattie tried to keep her garden alive by carrying water to it in buckets, but the best she could do was coax a stunted crop from it.

The corn was ready to harvest in June. Ike got only about one-third of what he had expected. The small savings he had brought with him from the sale of his share of the grocery and dry goods store dwindled faster than he could believe. Mattie began to cook more dried beans and less canned meat.

In spite of the hard times, or maybe because of them, the people at Santa Rita organized a picnic to celebrate the Fourth of July. All the families that had bought land attended, though most of them were hard pressed to find food to feast on. Mattie took fried chicken, deviled eggs, and light bread. There were lots of vegetables from Mr. Sponsellor's artesian-well-watered garden. And there were kegs of cold beer, furnished by the people who organized the picnic. Helen had not tasted it before. She dipped a fork into her father's cup, licked it, and declared, "That's the worst tasting stuff I ever put in my mouth!"

For most of the northerners, this was their first time to enjoy any kind of social contact since they had come to Texas. Everybody had fun. Neville Hinnant was courting one of the Meade girls. Ike, though not a drinking man, had a little too much beer that day. And so did some of the other people. It was the only time Helen had ever seen her father tipsy.

CHAPTER THREE

July was cotton-picking time. All the Sewells except Emil went to the field. Ike and the three girls picked in regular cotton-picking sacks that they dragged on the ground behind them. Mattie preferred to pick in a clothes basket. She picked only where the plants were biggest and fullest of bolls, and she picked more cotton in a day than anybody else. Harold picked in a pillow case, and when he got enough for a pillow, he often went and lay with his head on it and went to sleep. Howard simply rode on somebody's sack—he was too little to pick. The yield was disappointing. Only the heartiest of the plants had survived, and they had produced only part of their potential. But the family did have a few wagonloads of cotton to take to market.

They piled the white, fluffy bolls on the ground until Ike figured they had 1,500 pounds. Then he brought the wagon, to which he had attached side boards, and they lifted the cotton by tubfuls and dumped it into the wagon. He covered it with a tarp and took it to Hebbronville to the gin. Fifteen hundred pounds would make a 500-pound bale. Ike took the seeds back home with him, to use for next year's planting, and also as feed for his horses and mules.

Mattie always packed him a lunch of fried chicken and light bread to take with him to town. He ate it while he fed his horses, on the lot behind Sixto Garcia's general store. Then, he'd go into the store and charge to his account anything Mattie had ordered. Mr. Garcia always gave him a few sticks of peppermint candy: "*Pilón* for the young ones." Along in the night, Ike's young ones would be awakened by the sound of his wagon clattering over the rutted road, and they'd pile out of bed and run to greet him, and to receive the precious *pilón*.

When the cotton was all picked and taken to the gin, Ike went to see Sixto Garcia, to settle his account. That first year, it took all the money he got for his cotton, plus a little more. He had to dig into his now nearly nonexistent savings. The coming year would be a lean one.

Orders from the wholesale place in Laredo were cut to a minimum—mostly green coffee beans and canned milk to go in the coffee.

By carrying a lot of water, Mattie could usually have some kind of vegetables growing in her garden, and that is what kept her family fed for the first several years they lived in Texas. When they needed variety she used any edible things she found growing wild. She made jelly from the little berries of the pincushion cactus, or scrambled eggs with wild gerkins, or cooked black Mexican persimmons down into a "butter."

Childhood

Helen talked her father into buying her a rope lariat. Some of the cowboys used plaited rawhide lariats, but she knew Ike couldn't afford one of those. She practiced until she could rope a post with a fair amount of accuracy. What she really wanted to do was rope an antelope. She persuaded Harold to climb into a cotton sack and crawl around in the cotton patch, hoping an antelope would be curious enough to come close. But the animals were too smart for her—they kept their distance. Mattie was upset with her for trying. She told her: "It was a good thing you didn't get it. What would you have done with one if you'd roped it? You could never have held onto it. And you might have got tangled up in the rope. Goodness. What will you be into next?"

Helen went back to practicing on the post.

One day an elderly Mexican came bearing a gift. He offered them a dressed antelope shoulder and the whole hide. At first Mattie was reluctant to accept it. She told him it was against the law to kill an antelope, but the old man didn't seem to understand her. Finally she succumbed to what she believed to be kindness. Besides, they needed the meat. When Ike came to the house he told her: "I think that fellow wanted to get rid of that hide. He knew he had broken the law." Nevertheless, Ike tanned the hide, and they used it as a rug for a long time. And Mattie cooked the meat, but none of them liked it very much.

Anytime there was a fire in the cookstove, there was hot water in the ten-gallon reservoir—for washing dishes, and for bathing. They usually took sponge baths during the week, but on weekends they bathed in a galvanized washtub. The girls carried the tub and the water upstairs, and when they were through with their baths they threw the water out the window.

Every Sunday, Ike roasted enough coffee beans to last for a week, and each morning he ground enough for that day. Ike and Mattie drank coffee with milk or cream at each meal. The children drank water.

As the droughty summer wore on, the northerners who lived in tents began to think of going back where they came from. It had been a disappointing and frustrating year. Mattie had worked hard to keep something growing in her garden. Bucket after bucket after bucket of water, no matter how hot and tired she was. She devised interesting ways of preparing the monotonous food she had to serve her family. She did it with fortitude, and with prayer. Mattie had great faith in prayer. And it did seem that her prayers were often answered—as when Ike had a note coming due and nothing to pay it with. He became very

CHAPTER THREE

depressed, but Mattie told him: "The money'll come. I'll pray about it." And the next day she considered her prayer was answered. A man from the large and well-known King Ranch came and bought almost all of the flock of guineas she had been building up. He paid her $50 for them. That was the amount that was due on Ike's note.

But it took all the faith Mattie could muster and then some to keep Ike feeling optimistic. When badly needed rain refused to come, for instance, he would sit in his old chair by the north side of the house, his corncob pipe in his mouth, gazing dejectedly out across the prairie. Sometimes he spoke of being afraid his family would starve. At times like this Mattie would go to her garden and work harder than ever. Then she would come to the house and put an appetizing meal on the table.

Mattie did all the cooking. She liked to cook. But she seldom washed dishes — she always found somebody else to do that. Helen got little practice in the art of cooking when she was growing up, but she got plenty of practice in the art of dishwashing.

It was an isolated life they led at Tipperary Farm. But Helen and Garland lived another life, vicariously, through characters in the stories they read in the old magazines and in the stories they told to each other. This other life took them to Osawatomie, Emporia, even to New York.

The magazines Uncle John sent often contained stories set in New York, with characters who led glamorous, sophisticated lives in beautiful houses. The illustrations that accompanied the stories — and the advertisements — showed young women dressed in lovely clothes of the latest fashion, doing interesting things.

Their own stories were like the episodes of a late twentieth-century soap opera. The plot followed the ups and downs in the everyday life of a group of characters — villains and saints — reacting to each other. They used the same main characters in all their stories — Hazel Hill and Lucien Stuart, who were sweethearts; Mrs. Hartzen, who was their older friend and confidant — plus various minor characters. Like the characters in the magazine stories, these imaginary people had beautiful manners, wore elegant clothes, lived in grand houses.

Certain of the characters belonged to Helen — when they were doing the acting Helen told the story. When the others were in the spotlight Garland told the story. When Helen was telling the story, her characters tended to win, and when Garland was telling it her characters triumphed.

Childhood

These stories were the central interest in the girls' lives during the first three and one-half years they lived in Texas, years during which they did not attend school. If they were working together, they kept a story going. If they were separated, they looked forward to finishing their tasks and getting back to their storytelling. They usually had no control over the time they stopped a story—when they'd be picking cotton and it came time to go to the house, when they were washing dishes and Mattie ordered them to get through with that so she could assign them to other tasks, when they were telling stories at night and Opal told them to stop keeping her awake. They often had to stop in the middle of a confrontation. Tune in tomorrow and see what happens. . . .

Helen and Garland longed for the kind of life their characters led. They told themselves they would go to New York someday and live that way. And in preparation for that they decided to start acting in a way they considered proper. They started saying "please," and "thank you," using correct grammar, and talking like the characters in the magazine stories. And each night before going upstairs to bed they'd go and kiss both parents good night.

This had been going on for a week or two when the girls—sitting on the stairs when they were supposed to be in bed—overheard a conversation between Ike and Mattie.

Ike said, "I think it's just a stage they're going through. They wouldn't both of them go crazy at the same time."

"Well, I don't know. We never thought Emil would act like he does," Mattie said.

"But the way the girls are acting is a far cry from the way Emil acts."

"Well, yes, it is," Mattie said. "But it's not natural, you know that."

"I know," Ike said.

The girls sneaked back to bed. They knew their parents were very worried about Emil. They didn't want to give up their new roles, but they didn't want to add to their parents' problems, either. They talked it over and decided to stop trying to be elegant.

By Thanksgiving that first year the Danhausers and the Sewells were the only northerners left. The Huffs, the Meades, and the five or six other families who lived in tents had gone. They had had enough of South Texas. They just went off and left their lands. They didn't have anything else to leave—only the Danhausers and Sewells had built houses.

CHAPTER THREE

Ike, too, had been ready to leave a few times. In fact, he had once wanted to pick up and move to Mexico. But when he suggested that to Mattie, she said, "Hit the pike! If you want to go, go. But I'm staying here." So that put an end to that. Instead of moving, he made arrangements to rent the Meade place and plant it in cotton.

That fall, Mr. Sponsellor gave Mattie two small orange trees. She planted them in the yard and kept them watered faithfully. Oranges were a favorite of Mattie's. She could almost taste the sweet, juicy fruit when she tended her trees.

In December there was no money to spare for any kind of Christmas things. But the three girls went cheerfully about "making do." Mattie had an old fur coat she was willing to sacrifice—she had no need for it in Texas. The girls decided to make teddy bears. Stuffed toy bears were popular at that time because President Theodore Roosevelt was said to have once saved a bear's life. They made a big one for Opal, two medium-sized ones for Helen and Garland, and two small ones for Harold and Howard. Emil didn't want a teddy bear.

Helen tried to think of something she could make for Emil, and finally decided upon a collar box. She found an empty shotgun shell box that she thought was about the right size, and as there were lots of small snail shells around the yard and garden she decided to make the box pretty by covering it with snail shells. She stuck them on with flour paste. She was pleased with the project until she ran out of snail shells. She spent a lot of time searching but could not find enough to cover the box. So she didn't feel she could give it to him. But he knew she was making it, and he kept asking her to finish it. It was one of the few things he showed an interest in. Nobody knew what he would do with it when he got it—he didn't have any collars to put in it. She never did finish it, because she couldn't collect enough snail shells.

They cut a sugarberry bush (*Celtis laevigata*), stood it in a corner of the sitting-bedroom, and pretended it was a Christmas tree. When Ike went to town, he brought back rock candy and popcorn, and they used that to decorate the tree. As they finished each teddy bear, they placed it, unwrapped, under the tree. There was nothing to wrap the gifts in, no way to keep anything secret.

They kept the sugarberry Christmas tree there in the corner of the room for a whole year; they couldn't bear to take it down.

Nobody could say that first year in Texas had been a good one for the Sewells. And 1909 started out on a discouraging note. Ike's horse

Childhood

Charlie died. That left him with one horse and one elderly mule. He told Mattie there was no way he could farm their land and the Meade place without more draft animals. So he ended up going in debt for a span of half-broken mules named Jake and Jenny.

Sometime in January Helen received a letter from Marguerite. It told of all the things Marguerite had received for Christmas, and of a party their class at school had. Helen wrote back and told Marguerite about all the fun she had making the teddy bears, and about the beautiful Christmas tree they had that was different from any Christmas tree they had ever seen. She told of the warm winter sunshine, and of how they could go barefoot all year. She went on and on about what a great place Texas was. And by the time she got through she almost believed it.

Sometimes on Sunday afternoons Helen would reread Marguerite's letters and look once more at Kyle's card and feel a twinge of loneliness. That mood didn't last long, though. Helen had a lilting spirit, and sunshine in her heart.

Food at the Sewell house was more monotonous than ever that winter. Ike's savings had dwindled to almost nothing, so they spent as little money as possible. They ate a lot of dried beans and corn bread made with water. They had chicken now and then, and eggs of course. And sometimes Ike would shoot a cottontail, or some quail or plovers. There were no deer there then, and the antelope were off limits. They had no hogs or cattle. They didn't have any place to run cattle except out on the open prairie where they would get mixed up with the range cattle already there, and Ike was reluctant to do that. And they didn't know where to get a start of hogs—people in South Texas didn't seem to raise many hogs. Mattie's garden produced most of what they ate.

They ran an account at Sixto Garcia's store in Hebbronville, but prices were high. Mattie ordered only bare necessities. She told Ike, "I want to be sure not to owe more than we'll get when we sell our next cotton crop." Mattie always left the actual buying to Ike, but her influence was felt, nonetheless, in the management of their affairs.

They could take their own corn to Hebbronville and have it ground into meal. But they had to buy flour and lard. Mattie tried to make butter out of oil from cottonseed, but it wasn't good. She salted it. It still tasted like cottonseed.

Come February, it was time to plant corn. The first time Ike hitched

CHAPTER THREE

the new mules to the riding plow they ran away with him. He did work them, but he was half afraid of them.

Helen had no fear of the mules. Besides, she was bored with walking behind the docile old mule she and Opal had been working. She kept asking Ike to let her try working Jake and Jenny. "Naw," he told her. "You couldn't handle them. Be a good girl, and just keep walking behind old Sam." Helen bided her time.

One morning, just as Ike and Opal were ready to start for the field, they heard Emil in a big argument with Mattie. Ike handed the reins to Helen and said, "Here. Hold these till I see what's going on in the house."

He hadn't said *where* to hold them, so Helen climbed on the plow and took the mules to the field. By the time Ike caught up with her, she was halfway on her second round. He could see she was having no trouble with the equipment, *or* the mules. To himself he said, "Huh!" He allowed her to make a few more rounds before he put her off the plow.

After the corn was planted, they started in on the cotton. They planted all of the Meade place in cotton, and before they were through Helen was handling the wild mules with ease.

That spring, they got rain when they needed it. The crops grew strong and healthy. Ike was happy. He went around singing. He had a good voice and had sung in the church choir in Kansas. Helen loved to hear him sing, and she often sang with him. It began to look as if their crop troubles were over.

Mattie's garden thrived also. She had to carry very little water to it.

But if things were going well at last, that didn't mean the Sewells were through with problems. Ike came in from the Meade place one day with a face as long as Helen's lariat. The cotton leaf worms had invaded his cotton patch. The family went to have a look. In some places the damage was extensive. Where the worms had done a lot of eating, a sweet, sickening smell filled the air.

Ike had once heard some men in Hebbronville talking about a poison that would control the cotton leaf worm. He and Helen headed for Hebbronville to buy some of that poison. It was called London Purple.

On the way back to the farm that night Ike and Helen experienced something both of them remembered for the rest of their lives. Whether it was as awesome as it seemed to them, there is no way to know. But the feeling was real to them that night, and it remained real every time they thought about it afterwards.

Childhood

The night was very dark. There was no moon. Ike told Helen, "I hope these mules have enough sense to stay in the road, I can't see a thing." Helen couldn't really see much of anything, either.

After a while they drove down into a small valley and were immediately enveloped in light. A weird green-yellow light. It was coming from fireflies. Millions and millions of fireflies, their little lights switching on and off, on and off—twinkle, twinkle, twinkle. The rains had produced an abundance of tall grass, and the fireflies must have found the conditions just right for them, too. The grass was full of them, the air was full of them. "It was like trying to drive through the Milky Way, like being up there with all those stars."

But the next morning they knew they were back solidly on earth. They faced a most disagreeable task. Ike mixed the London Purple with flour, put the mixture in cloth flour sacks, and early in the morning, while the dew was still on, he took Helen and Opal and went to the cotton patch. He himself took a couple of sacks and gave the girls a sack for each hand, and they went up and down the rows, shaking the purple poison onto the cotton plants. By the time they stopped for the day they were as purple as the plants. It got in their eyes, and in their noses. They spat it out of their mouths. It took them several days to work all of the cotton. The girls hated the job. But it saved the crop.

The cotton boll weevil that crossed from Mexico into the lower Rio Grande counties of Texas in the early 1890s had by 1909 spread to the Hebbronville area and had already begun to be something of a problem. Helen wrote a poem about it.

The Little Boll Weevil

Where does the little boll weevil go
About the time it starts to snow—
Way down in Texas in a cotton boll.
Rolled in cotton, packed into bale
Put on the platform for sale.
Who'll buy the little boll weevil?

CHAPTER FOUR

Word about the successful Fourth of July picnic held at Santa Rita in 1908 got around. For the Fourth of July, 1909, one was planned at neighboring Las Vívoras, the ranch owned by Ralph McCampbell and his wife, Ella. Las Vívoras was maybe seven or eight miles from Santa Rita. Ranchers and their families came from all over the area. People came from Hebbronville. A few came from the little town of Alice, about fifty miles north of there. It was a big affair.

The picnic was held by a small lake, or pond, under a grove of hackberry trees. That in itself was a rare treat—trees were scarce in that country in 1909, but hackberries were a type of tree that could sometimes be persuaded to grow there, with plenty of water.

Ike had a big patch of watermelons that year, and he took a wagonload to the picnic. Mattie took fried chicken, potato salad, light bread, and pickles and preserves made from watermelon rind. People brought lots of pies and cakes.

Ice could be bought at Edds and Acklen Lumber Company in Hebbronville then—it was shipped by train from Laredo. A Mr. Allen brought a 100-pound cake of ice to the picnic and made a big freezer of ice cream.

There were horses to ride. Mrs. McCampbell's niece, Ruth Dinn, who was about Helen's age, was there from Alice, and she and Helen rode horses "like wild Indians" most of the afternoon.

Helen recited poetry for the group.

There was a baseball game.

In the evening there was music and dancing.

The Sewells met two families that day who would become important to them: the William Davids and the E. L. Armstrongs.

When the cotton was picked in July, Ike sold enough to pay their bill at Sixto Garcia's store plus enough to buy shoes for all the family

Childhood

and some money to add to the savings account. Everybody was happy. Especially Helen. She talked her father into buying her some red shoes that she assured him were the only pair in the store that fit her.

Even if Helen had been willing to accept a more mundane color of shoes, she probably could not have found a pair that fit well without going to Laredo. Mr. Garcia's stock of shoes tended to run in small sizes because the bulk of his shoe trade was with Spanish-American women and children and all of them had small feet. Helen's feet were long and narrow. She jammed them into the lovely red shoes—and got bunions.

The Danhausers were not faring as well as the Sewells. For them, 1909 was even more disastrous than 1908. They did not poison their cotton, and the worms destroyed most of it. That fall they went back to Kansas. Now, of all the families who had bought land in the Santa Rita area, only the Sewells were left. The Sponsellors still lived at Santa Rita, but the Sewells saw little of them.

Helen and Garland continued to tell their stories to one another. And Helen carried on a regular correspondence with other young people through "Cousins' Corner" in the San Antonio *Semi-Weekly Express*. She signed herself "South Texas Cowgirl."

That Christmas they replaced the year-old sugarberry tree with a fresh one and decorated it with popcorn and peppermint candy canes. No gifts were in evidence. But Ike went to Hebbronville the day before Christmas. A feeling of expectation was in the air. And when he came home, he had oranges and mixed nuts to put under the tree, and three nannie goats and a billy to turn into the yard. The children were excited. Helen claimed the ugliest of the nannies "because it was the smartest." Opal and Garland claimed the other two.

It promised to be a merry Christmas.

But the next day Mattie discovered that the goats had eaten all the bark off her orange trees.

They kept the goats—it was too late to save the trees. Mattie never did try to have any more orange trees.

One day that spring Mattie had a miscarriage. Opal and Helen were at the house at the time. Opal said, "Mama's fainted. Go get Papa."

Helen ran to the field screaming, "Mama's dead. Mama's dead. Mama's d–e–a–d. . . ."

By the time Ike and Helen got to the house, Mattie was conscious, and obviously embarrassed and annoyed. She ordered all of them out of the room.

34

CHAPTER FOUR

That spring, Ike said anybody who wanted to plant and tend twelve rows of cotton could have all the money those rows brought. The three girls took him up on it. Even Garland planted and cared for her twelve rows—with a little help from Helen.

There was much about Halley's comet in the San Antonio *Semi-Weekly Express* that spring. Ike became excited about it and insisted the girls read aloud every word of it so the little boys could hear about it, too. He was disappointed that they did not read as well as he had expected them to. He told Mattie, "They don't read as well as they did a couple of years ago."

Mattie said, "Oh, well, don't worry about it. Alleene will be here next year and she can teach them. They're smart. They'll catch up quick."

In April Ike got them up to watch the comet, every night. There were no trees or hills to interfere with the view. It was spectacular. Ike insisted that his family participate fully in what he felt would be a once-in-a-lifetime experience. Helen did. And she remembered it vividly ever after. "Looking eastward, the head seemed to be a few feet above the horizon, and its tail spread fan-like all over the heavens. I reached up toward it and tried to let the rays shine on my hand."

When cotton was ready to harvest, Helen went with Ike one day to take a load to the gin, and on their way home a bobcat ran across the road in front of them. The mules started to run. Ike yelled at Helen, "They're gonna upset the wagon!"

Helen could see that her father had lost control of the mules. She reached out her hand and said, "Give me the reins."

He did, and immediately lay down in the bed of the wagon.

Helen knew she could not stop the mules, now that they were running with all their might. She concentrated on trying to keep them in the road. Finally they wore themselves out, running like that, pulling the wagon through that deep sand. She didn't have any trouble with them the rest of the way home. Ike got up and sat beside her. But he let her drive.

Ike decided the answer to his problem of wild mules would be to breed Nellie to a jack and raise his own mules and start controlling them as colts. Nellie raised big, handsome mules for many years. He had not thought he would like to work mules—he had always liked draft horses. But he became very proud of those mules of Nellie's.

The three nannie goats had kids. One of them gave more milk than her kid needed, so Mattie told Helen to milk enough for coffee cream.

Childhood

Garland had to hold the goat's horns while Helen milked. Sometimes the girls would sneak a drink of milk before they took it to the house.

After the cotton had all been picked and sold, the three girls put the money from their thirty-six rows together and bought an old cow pony with bridle and saddle. Now they had transportation. His name was Sancho. They rode him around in the area, and to Santa Rita to pick up mail.

That fall Ike borrowed a big scoop and hitched a span of mules to it and dug himself a pila. He situated it so it would catch the overflow from the well. On the ranches of South Texas pilas were used as swimming holes as well as for watering livestock. The Sewell youngsters swam in theirs. That was where they learned to swim.

In the spring of 1911 Ike's father died, and Ike inherited $3,000 from his father's estate. Instead of paying off the note on Tipperary Farm, or buying the Meade place, which he wanted, he used the money to buy a bunch of untamed horses from Reuben Holbein, and turned them loose on the prairie. He thought he was going to make a lot of money selling their colts, that they wouldn't be any work for him, they'd take care of themselves.

But he soon learned that those horses were going to be more trouble than he expected. They ran into the barbed wire that fenced the Meade place, Tipperary, and Santa Rita. Sometimes they broke the fences. Some of the horses got cut on the wire, and the wounds became infected.

There was no veterinarian in Hebbronville then. Ike could not have rounded up the wounded horses and penned them, anyhow. He had no experience with that sort of thing. Some of the horses died. Ike had to start mending fences. And this at a time when he needed to be tending his crops.

He had Helen helping him fix fence one day, and a strand of wire slipped when he was stretching it. Helen's arm was badly cut. She bled profusely. Mattie stopped the bleeding by applying a layer of spider's web and bandaging the arm with a piece of an old pillow case.

Mr. Sponsellor told Mattie that if she and her children would help him put out his crop of Bermuda onions that spring, he would give her a garden plot there at Santa Rita, and enough onion sets to plant it, and allow her to irrigate it with water from the artesian well. She was glad for the chance. Ike had been wanting to grow onions. Now they could, without spending any money, and without carrying any water.

CHAPTER FOUR

The onions grew well. The crop was big. And those onions were delicious. But when the Sewells harvested them, they didn't know what to do with them. Ike tried to sell them in Hebbronville, but nobody wanted them. He felt sure he could sell them in Laredo, but no one there wanted any onions from Hebbronville—they grew onions all around Laredo, even shipped them out from there. So, there was no market for Mattie's onions. She cooked them, every way she could think of. She creamed them, fried them, baked them, made onion soup. The children ate them raw, like apples. But what they used could not even be missed.

Mr. Sponsellor couldn't sell his onions, either. Finally he and Ike decided to store all the onions in the upstairs of the Danhauser house. That house was vacant. The Danhausers were not coming back. And nobody else was likely ever to live there. Anyway, the onions wouldn't hurt it.

Alleene received her teacher's certificate from Kansas State Normal School that spring, and she came to Texas. It was an exciting time for the family. Alleene was eager to see this place she had heard so much about, and the rest of the Sewells were eager to show it to her. They all did a lot of visiting, and catching up, during those first days. And once Helen overheard a conversation between her mother and her big sister. Alleene said, "Helen seems to have grown into quite a young lady."

"Yes," said Mattie, "but she hasn't changed. Do you know what I caught her doing one day? Trying to rope an antelope! She could have been killed. Sometimes I don't know what to do with that girl. Trying to keep a rein on her is like trying to tame the wind."

Alleene said, "Oh, Mama. Helen's all right."

Mr. Sponsellor and Ike thought of another use for the Danhauser house. It would make an excellent schoolhouse. It was about halfway between the Sewell farm and Santa Rita. The Sponsellor and Sewell children could walk to it. With four young Sponsellors and four Sewells, they would have enough students so that the state would pay a teacher's salary if the parents would provide a schoolhouse. And they had a ready-made teacher in Alleene.

Opal, Helen, Garland, and Harold went to school that fall, after being out of school for more than three years.

On their way from Tipperary Farm to the Danhauser house Alleene and the younger Sewells walked through a small grove of trees that

Childhood

grew around a pond. This was the only place on that part of the prairie where trees grew. There were hackberries, retamas, and a few mesquites and huisaches, and there were always lots of birds flitting around. The young people loved to linger there. Helen considered the place enchanted. For a while, anyway, she felt transported to a different land—where nymphs and elves peeped from behind the tree trunks, and fairy princesses trailed their cobweb gowns through the cool shade. The few trees would have provided firewood for at least a while, but Ike did not wish to cut them. None of the other families had violated them, either—it would have seemed sacrilegious—these were the only trees anywhere around there that existed without the help of man.

Ike kept losing horses. Finally he decided to sell what he had left of them back to Mr. Holbein.

Alleene and Opal wanted two of those horses. They told Ike that if he would allow them to keep a couple of the two-year-olds, they would work and pay for them. And when the man came to get the horses, the girls selected two and asked him to put them in the corral for them.

By now, Opal and Helen knew how to handle a horse. So the girls broke the two horses to ride. They did it by being gentle with them. They saw to it that every mouthful of food the horses got came from one of the girls. Sometimes they sneaked a little sugar for them. Eventually they eased a bridle on one of them, bribing him with sugar. When they got both of them to allow the bridle, they eased a saddle blanket on, and finally a saddle. When Helen climbed on Alleene's horse—they named him Prince—he bucked a little but she stayed on him, and the next time she got on him he bucked less. Opal's horse was named Dandy. He didn't like to be ridden, either, at first. But Opal never allowed him to throw her. It wasn't long before all the girls were riding the two fine horses, with ease.

To own the Meade place was still one of Ike's goals. He used the money he received from the sale of the horses to make a down payment on it. But what he got out of the diminished herd of horses was considerably less than he had paid for them.

As the fall wore on, school seemed to be going well. Ike told Mattie it looked as if he had lost his field hands. He started looking for some Mexican help. It was not easy to find. There were not many unemployed Mexicans in that part of the country in 1911. The series of revolutions that started in Mexico in 1910 and lasted off and on for

CHAPTER FOUR

more than a decade, and that caused an influx of Mexicans into Texas, had not as yet had an effect on the area around Hebbronville. The term *wetback* had not been invented then, because not until 1917 were there any restrictions on border crossings for either Mexicans or Texans. Ike, however, was able to hire a newly married couple named Reymundo and Librada. They had grown up in Randado, the historic Spanish plantation and trading village about fifteen miles to the south.

Ike built his new help a small house on Tipperary Farm. They were happy, outgoing people, and the Sewell youngsters enjoyed visiting with them. It wasn't long before they were all chatting away in a variety of the Spanish language known as "Tex-Mex."

Shortly before Christmas that year Emil ran away. Well, what he probably did was walk away. He was so crippled it was very difficult for him to run, though he had been trying to run in the yard recently. It was on a day when the rest of them were busy with their own affairs. Mattie and little Howard were in the garden, Ike was in the field with Reymundo and Librada, and of course the others were in school. They didn't miss Emil until evening. They didn't know how long he had been gone.

The whole family started searching, and they kept on searching into the night. It was one of those exceedingly hot winter days that presage a storm. After a while the temperature fell and it began to sleet. Ike called them in and said they'd have to stop until morning. Mattie was determined to keep up the search. Ike took her gently by the arm and sat her on a chair and looked directly into her eyes and said, "No, Mat."

She looked at him for a few seconds, heaved a sigh, and sat still.

The next morning Ike went to Hebbronville and asked for help. Men came and searched for many hours. Finally they found Emil, most of his body submerged in a big trough where a windmill pumped water continuously for the range cattle. He was ten miles from home.

Perhaps the water, which was much warmer than the air at that time, kept him from freezing. He was alive. But he was in bad shape. He had left the house dressed in a short-sleeved shirt and cotton trousers. And sometime during his ordeal he had eaten tunas, the fruit of prickly pear cactus, spines and all.

Mattie got him cleaned up and did her best to get the spines out of his lips and tongue, and things settled back more or less to normal for the Sewell household.

Childhood

Then, one day Neville Hinnant came driving a part-Jersey cow and calf. He said he thought the cow had been accidentally left when some of the other northerners moved away, that he knew she did not belong with the cattle he was herding. He thought the Sewells might as well have her.

He couldn't have brought them a better gift. Mattje said, "Goodness! And I hadn't even prayed for one."

Alleene organized a Christmas program at school. Part of it was a play in which a boy went to the dentist to have a tooth pulled. None of the boys wanted to take the part, so Helen volunteered to be the boy with a toothache. She didn't have any boy's clothes that fit her, but Mrs. Sponsellor loaned her a brand-new pair of pants that belonged to her son Virgil. Virgil was about Helen's age, and the pants fit perfectly.

In the play, the boy with the toothache was supposed to be so afraid of the dentist that he jumped out the window when the dentist came into the room. Helen got so tickled when she did this that she wet her pants. Or, rather, she wet Virgil's pants.

The Danhauser house made an excellent schoolhouse except for one thing—the onions Ike and Mr. Sponsellor stored upstairs began to rot. The children and Alleene held school the rest of the year in a "fragrant" atmosphere.

For Christmas the Sewell children received tablets and lead pencils. Helen used hers to write a short story. It was called "The Uninvited Guest," and it was about a ranch woman who was frightened in the night by a calf that had walked into the house. Most farm and ranch houses had no screen doors at that time, and in hot weather the wooden doors were often left open. Helen submitted the story to the San Antonio *Semi-Weekly Express,* and they published it. That led her to assume she was now an established writer.

Feeling it would be selfish to keep all the fame for herself, she decided to be nice and allow Garland to share it. Together they wrote a story and sent it off to Grosset and Dunlap Publishing Company in New York, a name and address they had gotten from one of the magazines Uncle John sent. And as this was the first thing they had submitted, they thought they ought to send a biographical sketch. They told their ages, said they were both in the fifth grade but that they planned to go to school some more, and that they could write lots more stories if the publisher wanted more.

The letter was simply appended at the end of the story, so when

CHAPTER FOUR

the publisher returned the manuscript with a rejection slip the letter was returned also. Alleene picked up the mail and was so curious about the envelope from Grosset and Dunlap that she opened it and read the contents. Helen and Garland were crushed. Not only had she invaded their privacy, she laughed at them, and teased them. "It made us so mad we cried."

All went well with the farming at Tipperary. Reymundo and Librada were good workers. Librada's father moved in with them, but he was too old to work in the fields.

One fateful Saturday afternoon Librada and her father walked across the prairie to Santa Rita to get some nice soft water for cooking beans. The water from the well at Tipperary was so hard beans would not get soft in it no matter how long they were cooked. The Sewells tried to keep water from either the Meade place or Santa Rita for cooking beans. So that morning Librada and her father had gone to fetch some.

Early that morning Ike had left Tipperary in a wagon, heading for Hebbronville, driving Nellie and one of her mule colts.

Reymundo was at the Meade place that afternoon, cultivating cotton. Helen and Garland were in the south forty, with the old mule Sam, trying to work the grass out of their own rows of cotton, when they became aware that Mattie was calling them. It was a good thing Mattie had a strong voice that carried well. She was telling them to come to the house immediately, that a storm was coming.

They obeyed their mother, as they were accustomed to do, but they did it at a leisurely pace. They had been telling one of their stories, and they continued to tell it as they started Sam toward the house. Sam stopped every once in a while to get a bite or two of grass — the cotton was grassy that year.

As the girls and Sam neared the house they saw Mattie out in the yard, waving her arms at them, urging them to hurry. Then they noticed that Reymundo came running in with Jake and Jenny. They looked at the sky. It was pink, and that meant hail. They finally began to hurry. Just as they and Reymundo ran onto the back porch the storm struck.

The back porch at the Sewell house was boarded up, completely enclosed except for one door. Ike had built it that way in order to have a good dry place to store his corn and cottonseed. The family gathered on that porch. The hail came down like shots out of a gun. It was not round like marbles or golf balls. It was jagged, elongated pieces

41

Childhood

of ice—like frozen splashes of water. And the pieces were big. The wind was strong. It broke every window out of the house. Hail covered the beds and the floors. It cut the hides of the mules and they bled. Mattie's garden was beaten into the ground, so she knew what the field crops would look like.

The family huddled in the safety of the back porch. They knew that Librada and her father, and probably Ike, were out there in the storm, somewhere. They were particularly worried about Librada because she was pregnant. Reymundo stood and pounded the wall and prayed.

Eventually it was over, and about that time they could see Librada walking toward them, carrying a battered lard can. Reymundo ran to her, and they held each other and swayed back and forth and cried. She said her father was "back there," someplace. He had taken off his coat and made her put it on. He told her to empty the water and put the lard can over her head and try to get home. Said he didn't think he could walk any farther.

Mattie was worried about Ike, but all she could do was worry. There were no telephones. She would have to wait until he came home, or somebody came to bring her word of how he was. She went with Reymundo and Librada to look for Librada's father. A heavy fog, or steam, rose from the ground and hampered visibility.

When they found the old man he was nearly buried in ice but he was still alive. Reymundo carried him to the Sewells' house, and Mattie heated water and put his feet in it. He chilled, and shook. "And his cheeks puffed out until he looked like a frog."

After a while Ike came home. He had realized the storm was approaching and had taken shelter at Santa Rita. When he saw the shape things were in around the place, he went out behind the house and sat in his old chair and hung his head. He didn't even smoke his pipe.

Mattie put the girls to work cleaning up the house. She said, "Be careful you don't cut yourselves on that broken glass. And make sure you get it all out of the beds." Then she went to the garden and raked the ice off a head of cabbage and came and built a fire in the cookstove and went about fixing her family something to eat. When she had them all at the table, she told Ike, "That ice will make the ground moist when it melts—you can plant more crops, and I can plant the garden again. It's a good thing it happened now, instead of when the cotton was ready to pick."

CHAPTER FOUR

A few weeks later, Librada gave birth to a beautiful, healthy baby boy that everybody adored. Helen often played with the baby and carried him around. Until one day Mattie discovered that Helen had lice in her hair. She had gotten them from the baby. To get rid of the lice, Mattie used a concoction made of vinegar and the red berries of the fishberry shrub.

The summer of 1912 was destined to bring important changes for the Sewell family.

CHAPTER FIVE

Neville Hinnant rode over to the Sewell place one evening and hitched his horse to the yard fence. As soon as Helen saw his face, she knew he was bursting with some kind of news. And so he was. He said Fowler and Rankin had sold Santa Rita.

"Well for goodness sakes!" said Mattie. "Why did they do that?"

"I guess it wasn't serving their purpose any more," Neville said, smugly.

He told them it had been bought by an old man by the name of Draper and his two married sons and that the whole family planned to live there.

"Do they have any children?" Helen wanted to know.

"I think they have two or three real young ones," Neville told her.

The Sewells had lots of questions, but Neville couldn't give many details—he hadn't found out much about it himself.

This certainly was interesting news, and the Sewells' curiosity was aroused, but they didn't realize then that it was going to concern them in any important way.

It was after they were all in bed that night, and most of them were asleep, that one of the ways the change in neighbors would affect them occurred to Helen. She sat upright in bed and said, "Alleene . . . Alleene! If the Sponsellors leave, what's gonna happen to our school?"

"There won't be one," Alleene said. "I'll have to look for a job."

"Couldn't you teach us here at home?"

"No. I have to make some money."

With that, Helen was out of bed and bounding down the stairs. "Papa! If the Sponsellors move, we won't have any school! Papa, what are we going to do?"

Mattie turned over and said, wearily, "Oh, Helen, go back to bed."

The next day Helen was at it again. "Mama, I want to go to school."

CHAPTER FIVE

Mattie told her, "Don't fret so. Papa will see what he can do about some kind of school."

Ike met the new neighbors and invited them to come to visit his wife. So one day Mr. Draper's two daughters-in-law, Myrtle and Tena, came with Tena's two small children—Dorothy and John, Jr.—and Myrtle's little Alfred.

While the adults visited on the front porch, Howard entertained the small Drapers in the yard. Three-year-old Dorothy came running back, all excited. "Mama! There's a chicken out there with beads all over its head!" She was speaking of one of Mattie's turkeys.

Helen stayed close to the adults. She was fascinated by Tena's flashing green eyes, and by the big diamond she wore on her finger. Helen couldn't remember ever seeing a ring like that. Every time Tena moved her hand the diamond sparkled in the sunshine. And the more Helen stared wide-eyed at the diamond the more amused Tena became, and the more her green eyes flashed.

That visit was the beginning of a long-lasting and close friendship.

Alleene started looking for a school to teach, and she found one on the Las Cuatas Ranch owned by Reuben Holbein, not more than fifteen or twenty miles from Tipperary Farm.

Pancho Villa's bandidos were active on the Texas side of the Rio Grande that spring and summer, gathering supplies for their campaign in the Mexican civil war. Every time Ike was in Hebbronville, men were talking about that. He listened with interest, but he really didn't worry about it. The raids seemed to be mostly on the larger ranches, especially those that had commissaries.

Then, one morning he was unable to find Nellie and one of her mule colts. They simply were not on the place. He went to Hebbronville and talked with the customs officers and the Texas Rangers. They told him they would be on the alert for Nellie and the colt, but they couldn't offer him much hope. Now, he had a different perspective of the bandit problem.

Some of the ranchers were moving their families to town for a while, and Ike decided to do the same. He rented a small, partly furnished house. Mattie and the children moved into it and lived there for several weeks, until the bandits became less active in the area. Ike remained on the farm with his Mexican help. As it turned out, the whole family could have remained there unharmed—nothing happened.

Living in town was not as exciting as Helen had supposed it would

Childhood

be. Hebbronville was dull. It was not so much that there was a lack of activity—every time a rider or wagon approached town all the dogs started to bark, and the roosters crowed, there was something going on all the time—but it was not the kind of activity that interested Helen. There was no place to go except the general store, and Helen didn't have any reason to go there; she didn't have any money to spend. With glamorous New York always just at the back of her mind, she wondered whether dusty Hebbronville would ever grow up to be a city.

But Hebbronville was trying. Until now it had not had a public school—the only school was a private Catholic one, taught in Spanish. But in the summer of 1912 the people of Hebbronville rented a building and made preparations to hold a public school the following winter, taught in English, enrolling any student of the area who wished to attend, Anglo or Mexican. They hired a teacher from Mission, Texas—a Miss Myrtle McHenry. She would teach first through eighth grades in one room. They didn't expect a lot of students in the higher grades, because many students, no matter what their ages, would be attending school for the first time in their lives.

While Mattie and the children were living in town, Ike inquired around until he found places for his children to live and work for their room and board, so they could go to school that winter. He placed Opal and Garland with Mrs. Henry Timberlake, who ran a boarding house. Harold stayed with the Henry Edds. And Helen went to live with Sheriff and Mrs. Oscar Thompson.

And another piece of good fortune came their way while Mattie and the children were living in town—the law enforcement officers found Nellie and returned her to them. They never did find the mule colt.

When the Sewells moved back to the farm, a warm friendship developed between them and the Draper family. The Sewell girls began to spend as much time as they could at Santa Rita. Besides Tena and Myrtle and their children, they got to know Tena's husband, John, and Myrtle's husband, Asa, and their older sister Docia. And they got to know the elder Mr. and Mrs. Draper.

Tena and Myrtle taught the girls to play a game of dominoes called Forty-two, and they in turn taught it to Ike. After that the Sewells played dominoes in the evenings on the kitchen table. Mattie didn't play. She usually went to bed and tried to go to sleep, but the noise from

CHAPTER FIVE

the kitchen kept her awake. She complained, but the game went on until ten or eleven o'clock almost every night. Ike was as bad about it as the girls. Nobody paid any attention to' Mattie.

That fall the children moved to their various living quarters in Hebbronville, to start school.

The Oscar Thompson home, where Helen was to live, was the most prestigious house in town, and Mrs. Thompson was considered the *grande dame* of Hebbronville. She was from New England. She had come to one of the towns along the river to teach school, and had met and married Oscar Thompson. Her father, who was a carpenter, lived with them. He had, in fact, built their imposing house, which had twelve rooms with five fireplaces, and screened porches all around the house. One of Helen's chores was to sweep those porches every morning before she went to school. They were always very dusty, because the house was near the shipping pens where hundreds of cattle milled around all the time.

Hebbronville was said to be at that time the largest original cattle-shipping point in the country. Herds were driven in from as far away as the Rio Grande fifty miles to the south. The pens were full all the time. The cattle were brought to the outskirts of Hebbronville and kept in holding areas called "traps" until they could be fed and watered and moved to the shipping pens. Almost any time, of any day, clouds of dust followed cattle and drivers down the deep sand of Main Street. In the Thompson house the bawling of cattle could be heard constantly.

In order to get all those porches swept before she went to school, Helen had to start early in the morning, while it was still dark. She swept by a lighted lantern until daylight.

Another one of her chores was to wash and polish the oil lamp chimneys each afternoon. The Thompsons kept a lamp in every room, so there were lots of chimneys to polish. Oil lamp chimneys are fragile things, and Helen often broke one, in spite of trying to be careful. It got to where Mrs. Thompson called her "Miss Drop."

Mrs. Thompson was outspoken, and strict, with everybody in her household. It took some time for Helen to become accustomed to her. Once she thought of leaving and walking the fifteen miles back to Tipperary. "I wouldn't have minded the walk, but I hated to have anybody see me leaving with my bag of clothes."

Another thing Helen was expected to do at the Thompsons was

Childhood

churn. They had a cylindrical churn that hung from the wall. She used a wooden handle to push it back and forth in order to separate the butter from the milk.

The Thompsons had two small sons of their own, and a fourteen-year-old Mexican girl named Chata whom they had adopted. The little boys went to school but Chata did not wish to go. "She preferred to stay at home and help Mrs. Thompson with the cooking."

And they had a woman named Lupe Garibay who did the laundry, by hand, out in the wash house.

Chata and Helen became good friends, and when Helen wasn't busy she would often be in the kitchen telling stories while Chata worked. One day they almost got into trouble when Mrs. Thompson walked into the kitchen at an inopportune time. Chata was kneading bread, and Helen was telling a story. Chata started acting silly and throwing the dough up and catching it. She threw it higher and higher until at last it hit the ceiling and stuck there. That was the minute Mrs. Thompson chose to walk through the kitchen. The dough began to come loose from the ceiling. Helen held her breath. Fortunately, Mrs. Thompson was out of the room before the dough came down.

Mrs. Thompson, too, became Helen's friend before the winter was over. She became Helen's mentor, and remained that for the rest of her life, doing many gracious things for Helen. Once she made her a lovely white dress, with lace, and ribbons pulled through insertion. But, much as Helen loved her, she never got over being intimidated by her.

Around three o'clock in the afternoon, all over Hebbronville the aroma of roasting coffee filled the air. Unlike Ike, who roasted enough beans at one time to last for a week, these people roasted only enough for one day. Even for Helen who didn't drink coffee, the smell was pleasing.

Miss McHency, the schoolteacher, also lived with the Thompsons. She created quite a stir in the dusty little cow town. Anybody who came to Hebbronville as a stranger was news in that isolated place. And if that stranger was a pretty young lady who began to date a local cowboy, but who received many letters from her hometown with a man's name as part of the return address, she came close to beating the weather as a topic of conversation.

Miss McHenry entertained her gentlemen friends in the swing on the front porch, and Helen and Chata entertained themselves by peeping from behind the window curtains.

CHAPTER FIVE

The cowboy fell in love with the schoolteacher, but when the school year was over she went back to Mission and married her hometown sweetheart. This broke the cowboy's heart. Helen composed a song to the tune of "Streets of Laredo," describing the sad state of the cowboy, and of a cowgirl who loved *him:*

The Streets of Hebbronville

As I walked the streets of Hebbronville one morning,
As I walked the streets that morning so fair,
I saw a cowboy all dressed in brown linen,
As if for the train he thought to prepare.
This cowboy's in love with a schoolmarm from Mission.
This cowboy's in love with this lady so fair.
But she is to be married soon to another
Who seems to her to be more dear.

I know a cowgirl in love with this cowboy,
Who would bitterly weep if she knew he were gone.
Tonight she's lonely as she rides her pony
Far o'er these moonlit prairies so drear,
Not once dreaming he'd left that morning
To stop the marriage with his lips stained with beer.

She sold the composition for fifty cents to Dick Jones, one of Hebbronville's prominent young men.

The constant bawling of cattle was not the only noise Helen had to get used to when she lived at the Thompsons. That winter the sound of cannon from Pancho Villa's forces as they waged their civil war in the northern provinces of Mexico could often be heard in Hebbronville.

School was held for six months, and when it was over the Sewell children went back to Tipperary. It might have seemed dull after the months in town except that the Drapers were at Santa Rita. The two families visited back and forth and played Forty-two.

The Sewell girls still worked in the field, but now that Reymundo and Librada were there, they didn't have to stay with it as closely as they did when they first came to Texas. They had more time to tell stories, and to visit with the Drapers.

One day Docia Draper found a handwritten note in the top of a freshly opened five-gallon can of lard. It said: "I am Lester Atkins. I am sixteen years old. I would like to correspond with the girl who

Childhood

finds this." And he gave an address in Houston. Docia and Alleene talked Helen into answering the note, and a lively exchange of letters followed. It was fun for Helen. She signed her real name to the letters.

When Miss McHenry married and went back to Mission, Hebbronville was left without a schoolteacher, so there was no school there the next year. But Ike was determined, with no small amount of prodding from Helen, to find a way for his children to continue their education. He got together with two other families and made arrangements for a school to be held on Ralph McCampbell's Las Vívoras Ranch. There was a building that could be used as a schoolhouse, about halfway between the headquarters of the McCampbell ranch and those of the Montalvo ranch. The Montalvo children could walk from their ranch. The Sewell girls could walk from the McCampbell ranch, where Ike planned to rent a bunkhouse for them to live in. And the Dud Davids' little girl Eavie could live with the Sewell girls and walk to school with them. The McCampbells' only child, Howell, was older and already in school away from home.

They hired a retired teacher, Miss Julia Gray, from San Antonio. Teachers who were forced to retire from city schools because of their age often went and taught on the ranches, extending their careers a few years. The girls felt luck was with them when they got Miss Gray. In some ways she was the best teacher they ever had. She had studied elocution and liked to encourage her students to practice it. Helen loved it, and became quite good at declamation.

Miss Gray lived with the girls in the bunkhouse. Opal did the cooking. And in the evenings Miss Gray supervised their homework.

The bunkhouse was small and would have been crowded if the three Sewell girls, Eavie, and Miss Gray had all been there all the time. But two things relieved the crowding: Eavie was hardly ever there because when her mother brought her on Monday mornings she usually cried until her mother gave up and took her back home with her. And Mrs. McCampbell offered Helen a bedroom in the ranch house if she would cook breakfast for the family and the cowboys, so Helen was not at the bunkhouse much except in the evenings. She ate her evening meal there and studied there. When she was through studying, she went to the house and went to bed.

There was a spare room in the ranch house where they kept a large pitcher of water for bathing, and Helen was accustomed to go there to get water for a sponge bath before she went to bed. One evening

CHAPTER FIVE

she went through her regular routine, and just as she was pouring the water a man raised up in the bed, pointed a gun that looked enormous in the moonlight, and demanded: "¿Quién es? ¿Qué quiere?"

Helen fled, flinging "excuse me" over her shoulder.

The man was a Mr. Villarreal. He had sold a large shipment of cattle and was carrying the cash with him, so he was nervous. He had stopped to transact some business with Mr. McCampbell and had been invited to spend the night. Helen didn't know he was on the place.

Lee Norton was a cowboy on the McCampbell ranch. He often carried mail between the ranch and Hebbronville, and he noticed who wrote to whom. He asked Helen how she had met her friend from Houston, and when he learned she had never seen Lester Atkins, he began to chide her about writing to somebody she didn't know. He told her it was dangerous. Helen tried to ignore him.

Gertrude Russell, a relative of Mrs. McCampbell, was visiting at the ranch, and one Saturday she and Opal and Helen rode the eleven miles to the depot in Hebbronville to pick up a package of newspapers for Miss Gray. Opal rode a horse named Caesar. Caesar tried to buck off every man that got on him, but he would let the girls ride him. Gertrude rode a pinto. Helen rode a strong-necked steel gray called Sultan, who was bad to run and hard to hold.

As Helen was the most experienced rider, they tied the bundle of papers behind her saddle. Sultan didn't like that. He tried to buck, and almost ran over some men who were talking in front of the depot. And when they started back to the ranch Sultan began to run. The package of papers bounced up and down, and that made him run faster. His neck was short and strong, and Helen could not hold him. She tied the reins around the saddle horn and let him run. On the way she passed Asa Draper. He yelled, "What's your hurry?" But she was gone before she could answer.

Sultan ran all the way back to the ranch. Helen knew he would stop short when they got to the corral, so she braced herself and got ready to jump. She landed on her feet but she didn't stay that way. When she picked herself up she was greeted by an audience that included Mrs. McCampbell and several cowboys. It had rained hard the day before and the damp sand was packed so hard that they could hear the running horse's hoofbeats long before Sultan and Helen arrived, and they had come out to see what was going on. They all applauded.

All the Sewells were at Tipperary for Christmas that year. Grandpa

Childhood

Linville — Mattie's father — had sent a barrel of apples from Missouri. They were the first apples they'd had since they came to Texas, and those apples in themselves would have made the holidays merry.

Mattie cooked lots of spinach, carrots, turnips, beets, and other vegetables from her garden, fried mounds of chicken, baked custard pies. And of course there was light bread with good fresh butter.

Alleene and Opal went horseback riding almost every day on their two fine horses. Helen and Garland played with the goats, told a few stories, and helped their beloved Ben kill a rattlesnake. All of them visited with the Drapers.

Ike and the girls played Forty-two every night. And Mattie didn't even complain.

It was a a happy time, with everything going well. Until . . . one afternoon Emil took a maul and scattered Ben's brains all over the back porch.

Mattie's good food went begging that night. Nobody was hungry. Even the Forty-two game wasn't any fun. They finally gave it up and went to bed.

And then at the supper table the night before the girls were to go back to school Emil asked Helen to pass him the platter of fried chicken. She picked it up and looked for a drumstick for herself before she passed it to him. He got up and caught her by the throat and began to choke her. She was already turning blue when Ike persuaded him to release her.

Ike did not hit Emil, or lay a hand on him. He simply spoke sternly to him. Emil was a man now, and when he was angry he had great strength. Ike probably could not have overpowered him. Ike never whipped his children, but when he spoke sternly to them they never even considered disobeying. Emil had been conditioned to obey when Ike spoke like that. He probably obeyed without thinking.

The next morning the girls left to go back to school.

A few days after that Ike took Emil to the new Jim Hogg County courthouse in Hebbronville and asked the court to commit him. He was sent to an insane asylum in San Antonio, and except for some time in a hospital, he stayed there the rest of his life.

Lee Norton had gone to his home in Tyler for the Christmas holidays, and he got back to the McCampbell ranch about the same time the girls arrived. He told Helen that when he was at home he told one of his friends about her and that person wanted to write to her. In a week or so she received a letter. It was signed Egbert Gilliland.

CHAPTER FIVE

Egbert said he was a friend of Lee's, that Lee had told him about Helen, and he would like to correspond with her. She discussed it with Lee, and started writing to Egbert.

Now, she was writing to two people she had never seen. "Well, our social life was so limited. By mail was better than nothing."

Egbert's letters turned out to be interesting. Helen found them enjoyable, and intriguing. There was a slight air of mystery about them.

CHAPTER SIX

That spring the McCampbells needed another hand at roundup, and Helen volunteered. She had not participated in a roundup before. Lee Norton looked her up and down and said condescendingly, "So you really think you can work cattle—from daylight to dark?"

"Who says I can't?" Helen retorted.

Mr. McCampbell gave her a cow pony that was smart and well trained.

It was an exciting time for everybody on the ranch. Mr. and Mrs. McCampbell no longer rode with the cowboys, but they followed along behind the camp wagon in a surrey. They would not have missed roundup.

By daylight on the appointed day Helen had cooked breakfast for the McCampbells and the cowboys and was by her horse, ready to ride. "The challenge was exhilarating."

There were hundreds of McCampbell cattle scattered over that open range. They all had to be brought in. The big calves had to be separated from the cows, the young males had to be castrated, and all the calves had to be branded. It was a long day of hard riding. At noon they went to the wagon in shifts, to a lunch of beans, meat, and pan (a bread cooked in Dutch ovens).

Helen found that herding cattle with an experienced horse was not all that difficult. Mostly, the rider just had to stay with the horse, and Helen knew how to do that. Rounding up cattle was fun. But she had to talk to herself to keep from leaving when the branding started. "The smell of burning hide and hair was something I tried to forget."

Helen continued to correspond with both Egbert Gilliland and Lester Atkins. And Lee Norton continued to pick at her about it. He seemed to know a lot about what was in the letters she received from Egbert. It was puzzling. She even began to wonder whether he himself might be writing them. It became more and more obvious that there was

CHAPTER SIX

something strange about those letters, and that Lee knew more than he was telling. She finally asked him what it would take to get him to explain it to her. He said, "I'll tell you if you'll give me a Yankee dime."

Helen took the words literally. She told him, "Mrs. McCampbell pays my dimes; you'll have to collect from her."

Lee laughed until he nearly fell over, and Helen realized she'd bumped into something else she didn't understand. She went and asked Mrs. McCampbell's help, and was embarrassed to learn that a Yankee dime meant a kiss.

She worried around with her problem for several days and finally came up with what she thought was a solution. She waited until she and Lee and the McCampbells were all on the porch one evening, and she told Lee she would give him the Yankee dime if he would tell her what he knew about those mysterious letters.

He told her the letters were not from a man at all, they were being written by his sister Frankie, that he had enlisted Frankie's help when he was at home during the holidays so he could prove to Helen that she was foolish to write to people she had never seen. Then he walked toward her, saying, "When do I get my Yankee dime?"

Helen was not too surprised—she knew something was strange about those letters. But she had no intention of giving Lee a kiss. She had made a plan. She thought she had outwitted him; she intended to impose a condition that he would not wish to comply with. She told him, "You'll have to collect right here, in front of Mr. and Mrs. McCampbell."

Lee grabbed her and kissed her, soundly.

Helen was mortified.

The McCampbells enjoyed the show.

Helen retired to her room to consider what could be done to shore up her dignity. She had lost that round.

And to make matters worse, in the next letter she received from Lester Atkins he said he was planning to come to see her. With the humiliating experience of the other letters fresh in her mind, she sat down and wrote to Lester and told she was not a girl, she was a boy, her name was not Helen, it was Harold.

There went her social life, right down the chute.

In March of that year Helen left school and went to Alice, Texas. Mrs. McCampbell's sister, Hortense Lynn, was having her first baby,

Childhood

and Mrs. McCampbell asked Helen to go up there and help her sister for a couple of weeks. Few things could have pleased Helen more than the chance to be in Alice for a little while. She hadn't been anywhere bigger than Hebbronville since they had come to Texas six years earlier.

While Helen was staying with the Lynns, a Mrs. Perkins, whose husband was a judge in Alice, asked her whether she would work for her, caring for her three small children. Helen wanted to do it because she wanted to stay in Alice. Hortense talked it over with Mrs. McCampbell when she came to see the new baby, and it was Mrs. McCampbell's opinion that if Helen took the job she should be allowed to attend high school. She said to tell Mrs. Perkins that Helen did not *have* to work, she had a home, but if she did take the job she should be required to baby-sit only after school.

Helen moved to the Perkins home and lived there for almost two years. She came to love the three Perkins children: four-year-old Dorothy, two-year-old Lucille, and Patty, who was a baby. She entertained them with stories she made up, with pictures she drew with chalk on the sidewalk. She rocked them to sleep at night.

Judge Perkins owned a Hupmobile, one of the three cars in Alice at that time, and he taught Helen to drive it. Cars had to be cranked then, but that didn't bother Helen. Her arms were strong, as a result of persuading all those mules to do her bidding.

When school started that fall, Helen found a family for Garland to live with, so she could come to Alice and go to high school. And back in Hebbronville Mrs. Henry Edds was arranging for Opal to attend the Baptist Academy at San Marcos. That meant that the three Sewell girls would be entering high school in the fall of 1914. Opal was twenty years old, Helen was eighteen, and Garland was sixteen.

Shortly after Helen started living with the Perkins family, there was a revival meeting at the Methodist Church. She wanted to take the vows and join the church, but she felt timid about walking to the front of the church and declaring her intention. She discussed the problem with Judge and Mrs. Perkins, and they arranged with the Methodist minister for her to make her commitment in his study. So she became a member of the church. She attended Epworth League on Sunday evenings and soon was taking part in the programs.

Celebrations in Alice were attended by people from the Hebbronville vicinity, and those in Hebbronville were attended by Alice people, so it was not surprising that word got around in both places about

CHAPTER SIX

people who excelled in certain skills. Helen's reputation for horsemanship probably got to Alice before she did. At any rate, when they were planning a parade before one of their baseball games in Alice, they invited Helen to lead it, riding Red Bird, a famous race horse owned by the prominent South Texas rancher T. T. East. Although the horse was nervous, all went well. Right behind Helen and Red Bird came the Texas Rangers on their fine horses. And behind them came lots of other people on horses. Everybody ended up at the ball game.

Three other girls talked Helen into going for a ride instead of staying at the game. Red Bird was prancing around. When he was in a crowd, he expected to race. They rode out of town a little way, and on the way back the other girls wanted to run their horses. Helen tried to talk them out of it because she could see that it might be difficult to control Red Bird. But they did run. And Red Bird left the others far behind as he raced, out of control, right through the middle of Alice. Helen lost her hat, then her scarf, then one slipper. Men, women, and children scrambled for cover. Helen leaned over on the horse's neck and whispered to him, begging him to slow down. But he didn't—not until he came to where the street ended. "Anyhow, I stayed with him."

Next door to the Perkins family lived Mr. and Mrs. P. A. Presnall and their five children: Homer, Mary, Alice, Pope Arthur, and Julia. Mr. Presnall was president of the bank in Alice. The Perkins children played with the Presnall children, and Helen and Mrs. Presnall became friends.

One day Mrs. Presnall asked Helen, "When do you ever find time to study?"

It was true that when Helen wasn't in school, or asleep, she was taking care of the Perkins children. Judge Perkins and his wife went out almost every evening. Helen had to try to get her homework any way she could, a snatch here, a snatch there. But she loved those Perkins children. It didn't seem too bad.

About the middle of Helen's second year in high school Mrs. Presnall told her she knew an old lady who needed somebody to live with her, and that if she wanted to have more time to study maybe she should consider changing jobs. So Helen left the Perkins family and went to live with Mrs. George Cox.

The Cox home was very different from where she had been living. It was extremely quiet. About the only noise was Mrs. Cox's breathing. She was an elderly widow who had a serious heart condition, and her

Childhood

raspy breathing could often be heard all over the house. "Some nights I'd be afraid she wouldn't live till morning."

Helen visited with her, gave her what care she needed, and still had plenty of time for studying. She even wrote a short story that winter. It was about a young ranch girl who fell in love with a horse thief. She called it "Daddy's Hummingbird," and when she finished it, she mailed it to one of Ike's cousins, Homer Croy, a writer who lived in New York. He wrote to her and suggested that she put the story in what he called "scenario form" and send it to him, and he sent her a magazine that was supposed to be helpful to her. But Helen was busy with other things and never did get anything more done with the story.

For one thing, she was writing a novel that she was surreptitiously passing around for her schoolmates to read during study period. She never did finish the novel. She put it and the short story in the bottom of her trunk and more or less forgot about them. Her life was changing rapidly. She was taking an active part in the Epworth League programs, and she was dating regularly.

She felt obligated to spend time with Mrs. Cox, who was kind and generous, but who was different from anybody Helen had ever known. She was always talking about death. She hoped for her own death—looked forward to it. She told Helen she could hardly wait until she got to heaven and had a chance to meet and talk with Matthew, Mark, and John, and especially with Paul. She said she had gone over in her mind exactly what she intended to say to them. She was obsessed with meeting all of these people; it was about all she talked about. "She didn't talk about getting up there and seeing any of her family."

Helen wanted to go to Tipperary for the summer, so Mrs. Cox's niece and her husband came to live with the old lady until Helen returned.

Helen and Garland had written home, saying they'd be at the depot in Hebbronville on a certain day. Then, a few days before they left Alice they decided to invite a couple of their friends—Thelma Pearce and Jewel Jones—to go home with them for a visit. Thelma and Jewel thought the girls should ask their parents whether it was all right to bring guests, but Helen and Garland assured them that Mattie and Ike loved to have company and that they wouldn't consider it any trouble. They said, "Mama doesn't need to know ahead of time. She can always make do."

If Ike was less than happily surprised to find four girls instead of

CHAPTER SIX

two when he met the train, he didn't show it. And if Mattie wondered what she'd do with visitors for an indefinite length of time, she didn't show it, either. They made the girls welcome.

But this was not the most convenient time for company. It had been dry for more than a year. Ike had lost most of two crops. Mattie's garden was poor. The animals and poultry had to live on what they could glean from the dry fields. Mattie, Ike, Harold, and Howard had been living mostly on mush and milk. And that is the diet she served the girls, except for breakfast, when they could usually have eggs, or oatmeal.

The visiting girls stayed about two weeks. Mattie never complained.

Alleene and Opal were at home also, and in spite of monotonous food and hard times it was an enjoyable summer. The girls rode horseback often, sometimes to the Draper's place at Santa Rita, where they played Forty-two.

Once Helen and Opal rode Prince and Dandy out on the prairie, with no destination in mind. They kept going until they came to the Holbein ranch fifteen or so miles from Tipperary. Mr. Holbein had a car then, and as they neared his ranch he passed them in the car. Dandy bucked with Opal—it was of no great concern, Opal stayed with him. The Sewell girls were accustomed to coping. They'd been practicing it most of their lives. They rode the sandy trails and the open prairie without fear. They enjoyed riding over the grasslands of the prairie. Even then, those lands were being invaded by the brush that would in later years take them over. Opal would be living in a city by then. But Helen would be living on the prairie, still coping.

Another time that summer Alleene and Helen went for a ride and got caught out on the prairie when a storm was approaching. The sky got dark and lightning flashed around them. The horses became excited and started to run. The girls wound up at the McCampbell ranch, where they spent the night. Of course there was no way to let Mattie and Ike know that they had reached safety. And everybody knew there were bandits roaming the prairies at night. In fact the girls did see a couple of strange horsemen, but everybody kept on riding and nothing happened. It was not a time or place for the faint of heart.

The Drapers moved to town, which all of the Sewells regretted. Besides being without a congenial family of neighbors, the Sewells would now have to go all the way to the Alta Vista Ranch headquarters to get their mail, a distance of maybe ten miles.

Childhood

Helen and Alleene also moved to town for a while that summer. They lived at the Viggo Hotel and worked for their room and board, to get away from the isolation of the farm. They were living at the hotel on the Fourth of July. The weather was beautiful that day. W. W. Flowers, the county attorney, and his friend Charlie Yeoman invited the two girls to drive out to the Jesús María ranch, about twenty miles down the Randado road. The ranch was owned by Wilbur and Josephine Allen and was one of the most beautiful places around there.

In those days people in that area had no way of knowing that a storm was approaching until it was upon them. There were no telephones, no radios. And so the four young people were innocent of the fact that their beautiful weather was about to give way to a hurricane.

Soon after their arrival it began to rain. The showers came and went. The people gathered in the lovely ranch house were not concerned except to be glad to see the rain. They played games. Mrs. Allen played the piano and they sang. As the afternoon wore on, the wind now and then blew harder. But it was not until the sky got black and the rain started coming in torrents that they knew they were in for a hurricane.

The four visitors who had dropped by for a pleasant afternoon were now forced to spend the night. To lighten their spirits, Helen gave some of her recitations. Mrs. Allen was impressed. She asked Helen where she planned to go to college, and when she learned that Helen didn't expect to be able to do that she said, "Well, you *must* go, somehow. It would a shame to waste all that talent."

That was the summer Mattie's pig got sick. They had not had any hogs since they left Kansas, but in the spring of 1916 Ike had come home one day with four young pigs. Mattie was very proud of them. They were almost grown by the end of the summer when one got something wrong with it. Ike said, "Looks like you're gonna lose it."

Mattie said, "No. It's gonna live. I'll pray about it."

The pig got well.

Mattie was beginning to acquire quite a reputation for answered prayers.

Mrs. Presnall wrote to Helen, telling her that Mrs. Cox—the old lady Helen had been living with in Alice—had died, and inviting Helen to live with the Presnall family during her senior year.

The Presnalls had just built a new three-story brick house. Helen roomed with Mary and assumed her own share of the chores of the house. She cleaned one of the bathrooms, braided Alice's hair each morn-

CHAPTER SIX

ing, and fixed all the school lunches from ingredients Polly, the cook, prepared.

Mary was dating Thomas Wise, whom she later married. He had a Ford car. Helen began dating John Lipps, a teller at Mr. Presnall's bank, and the four double dated much of the time, using Tom's car. They occasionally drove the ten miles to San Diego on a Sunday afternoon, returning in time to attend Epworth League at the Methodist Church, where Helen often had a part in the program.

The Presnalls owned a Cadillac touring car, and they sometimes took the family to football games in Corpus Christi. It was Helen's first opportunity to see anything in Texas that could be called a city. And all that water! Helen thought of her mother, carrying water to her garden in buckets.

There was a wide ledge outside some of the windows on the third floor of the Presnall house, and Mary and Helen took drawing paper and water colors and climbed out on the ledge one day, and each painted a picture of the town of Alice. Some of the younger children climbed out there the next day, and Mrs. Presnall caught them and punished them. But she didn't catch Mary and Helen—they got away with it.

That winter there was a lot of talk about the war that was going on in Europe, and that was later to be known as World War I. Helen didn't really worry about it. President Wilson had promised—during the election campaign—to keep the United States out of other people's wars. Germany and France and all those other places were a long way from Alice, Texas. But then, on April 6, 1917, the United States declared war on Germany, and Europe didn't seem so remote any more.

Mrs. Presnall's brother Buddy was in the Navy, and he came to the Presnall house on leave in the spring of 1917. He was tall and handsome. "And all the girls in town were after him." He noticed Helen. And Helen noticed that he noticed her. But she was dating Johnny Lipps, and she and Johnny and Mary and Tom Wise were always running around in Tom's car. Buddy did not ask Helen for a date. But one day when they met on the stairs, he embraced her and kissed her. He still didn't ask for a date.

Helen had a trunk that she kept all her things in. It was in the room she shared with Mary. One day, in the tray of her trunk, she found a letter from Buddy. He said he would have to leave soon to go back to his ship, and he didn't know when he would be back. He said his sister thought a lot of Helen, and he could see that she was the

Childhood

kind of girl he wanted to marry when he got out of the Navy, and he asked whether she would consider being engaged to him now, and marrying him when he came home. He asked that she answer the letter and leave it in the trunk. And he asked her not to tell anybody.

Well. That was thrilling. Helen and Johnny were just friends at that time. She didn't know much about love. But she thought it would be exciting to be engaged. She answered the note and said yes. She and Buddy had a few more meetings on the stairs and he was gone.

Helen continued to go around with Johnny.

Students from some of the high schools in that area attended a speech meet in Alice that spring. Helen gave a dramatic reading of Susan Coolidge's "Ginevra" and won second place. Her former teacher, Miss Julia Gray, was teaching on a ranch near Alice then, and she coached Helen.

Weeks passed after Buddy went back to his ship, with no communication from him. Helen wondered about it, but she didn't worry. She was dating Johnny. Then, one day a friend told her she had seen several letters in the dead letter box at the post office addressed to Miss Helen Marie, with no last name, and she wondered whether those letters might be meant for Helen. Helen went to investigate and found the letters were indeed for her—they were from Buddy. He had forgotten her last name. Helen made the mistake of telling Mary about the letters, and she in turn told her mother. Mrs. Presnall was not pleased. She told Helen that Buddy was not a suitable sweetheart for her, that he had a girl in every port. Helen wrote to Buddy and called off their engagement, and told him why. Buddy became angry with his sister, and then she became angry with Helen. Helen wished she had never gotten mixed up in that.

Johnny was drafted into the Army in April. Before he left he proposed, and Helen accepted. She was engaged again.

Helen and Garland graduated from Alice High School that spring, and Opal graduated from the college preparatory school of the Baptist Academy in San Marcos. Garland was valedictorian of her class, and that got her a one-year scholarship to the Southwestern University at Georgetown, Texas. Mrs. Edds was instrumental in getting Opal a scholarship to the Baptist Academy.

It was an important time in the lives of the Sewell girls. Mrs. Presnall had a lovely organdy dress made for Helen's graduation. Johnny came to Alice for the occasion, and he and the Presnalls drove Helen

CHAPTER SIX

home a few days after it was over. Garland had gone home by train immediately, in order to be there to help Mattie prepare for the guests.

There was much entertainment: a lunch at W. W. Jones's Alta Vista Ranch followed by dancing on the large gallery, a picnic in the sand dunes just outside of Hebbronville. Johnny carved Helen's and his own initials on the hackberry tree in the Sewell yard and challenged Helen to find them.

Mrs. Josephine Allen had not forgotten how favorably impressed she had been by Helen's recitations the night of the hurricane, and she was determined to see that Helen got to college. Mrs. Allen's father, John Houghton, was a wealthy man, and a fellowship had been set up in his name at the University of Texas. It had been awarded for the first time the previous year, to Walter Woodall of Alice. Mrs. Allen set about to pull some strings. She succeeded in getting the John Houghton Fellowship awarded to Helen for the school year of 1917–1918. It was a loan of $300 at 3 percent interest.

Mrs. Allen also made arrangements for Helen to live with her mother-in-law, Mrs. Fred Allen, who had a house near the campus.

When Mrs. Presnall learned Helen was to go to college, she had several more dresses made for her to take with her. Alleene bought her a coat suit and paid her train fare.

In the fall of 1917 Helen was off on what was up to then the greatest adventure of her life.

Independence

CHAPTER SEVEN

In 1917 the University of Texas campus consisted of forty acres of land, in the center of which sat Main Hall and the Woman's Building, the Law, Engineering, and Education buildings, "B" Hall, and the beautiful library. Scattered around were a number of wooden structures referred to as "shacks." Some of the shacks were temporary dormitories; some housed classrooms. The latter were unadorned, long rectangular structures with a hall down the middle and classrooms along each side. Main Hall was not all that elegant, either—its floors had splinters that literally pierced the soles of shoes. But to the girl from Tipperary Farm it all looked big and grand.

Mrs. Fred Allen had a retarded daughter, and Helen helped pay for her room and board by sometimes looking after her. Helen looked after the daughter, and Mrs. Allen looked after Helen, feeling it was her duty to chaperon and advise her.

Helen wanted to study art, drama, and music, but she knew this one year was all the college she could expect to get. She felt she had to come out of there with a teacher's certificate, and to do that in one year meant she must fill her schedule almost entirely with education courses. So she buckled down. "But, oh, how I longed for those other courses."

Her classes were not necessarily dull, however. Walking into the zoology lab, for instance, was like landing on another planet. She had never seen a microscope. And all those specimens in bottles! She kept her eyes and ears open and tried to act sophisticated.

On the Friday they were asked to draw a crayfish from a specimen preserved in formaldehyde, Helen, thinking the liquid surrounding her specimen looked dirty, poured the formaldehyde down the sink and replaced it with nice clean water before she stored the specimen. When she open her locker at the next lab session, the odor drove the class out of the room.

Independence

Helen's counselor was sympathetic to her need for something besides education courses, and managed to include a public speaking course in her schedule. It was held in the basement of the Law Building, and Helen was the only girl in a large class of young men. Everybody, including the teacher, treated her with respect. She enjoyed it more than any other class, and made A's in it. But, alas, it was not to last. The young professor, like many of his colleagues in 1917, was drafted into the Army. The second semester of the class was canceled. The students organized and planned to continue without a teacher. Helen made the mistake of telling Mrs. Allen about this, and that lady, believing it improper for a young woman to be in class with all those boys and no teacher, ordered her to drop the class. Helen, afraid of losing her domicile, did as she was told.

Next door to Mrs. Allen lived a zoology professor and his teenaged son. One day the boy was playing with a rare coachwhip snake in the front yard, and he allowed Helen to hold it. A couple of girls came down the sidewalk while she was admiring the snake. "Those girls got pretty excited—they ran away shrieking."

Helen and the zoologist's son became friends, and the boy gave her a squid one day. One of her education classes had become boring, so she took the squid to school and threw it down a row of seats, over the laps of several girls. That also caused a certain amount of shrieking.

Helen had started school in the fall with the $300 she received from the John Houghton Fellowship fund, and at the end of the first semester she still had more than half of it. Mrs. Allen charged her only $10 a month for room and board, and Helen had been very careful of the way she spent her money. She decided to splurge and buy a book of student tickets to campus activities such as lectures and concerts. But after she attended one concert, Mrs. Allen refused to allow her to go again. She said Helen needed all of her time for studying.

With $115 of the original $300 still in her pocket, Helen returned to Hebbronville the last of May with a four-year first-grade teaching certificate. If she taught four consecutive years, the certificate would become permanent. And she planned to do that. Opal and Garland received certificates of the same kind that spring. Now, all four Sewell girls were schoolteachers. It had not been easy. But they had been determined. However, the two Sewell boys, Harold and Howard, did not seem to be that dedicated to learning.

Ike and Mattie were concerned about the boys' education, though,

CHAPTER SEVEN

Helen in riding habit, c. 1914.

Independence

Garland in riding habit, c. 1914.

CHAPTER SEVEN

Mrs. Ralph McCampbell at Las Vívoras Ranch, c. 1914.

Independence

Helen, Alleene, and Garland in pila at Tipperary Farm, summer of 1916. *Below:* Helen, Garland, and Alleene at Santa Rita, summer of 1916. Alleene is holding Opal's horse, Dandy.

CHAPTER SEVEN

Helen with two calves, at Tipperary Farm, c. 1916.

Independence

Helen with Johnny Lipps, beside the Presnall house in Alice, Texas, 1916.

CHAPTER SEVEN

Helen, summer 1916.

Independence

Helen at wheel of model-T Ford. Mrs. Ralph McCampbell in front seat, Garland Sewell in back seat. Probably around 1916.

CHAPTER SEVEN

Helen, in dress Mrs. Presnall had made for her high school graduation.

Independence

Helen and her colleague, Miss Edna Pentecost, in front of the new brick school building, fall of 1918. *Below:* Mrs. Jack Miles, Howard Sewell, Mary Hoffman, and Helen and her deer. (Mrs. Miles is supposed to be the author of the poem about the harsh environment and about Pell's trying to get himself a bride.)

CHAPTER SEVEN

Texas Ranger P. B. Harbison beside Edds and Acklen Lumber Yard, Hebbronville, about the time he and Helen met.

Independence

and in the fall of 1917 when they saw an opportunity to move to Hebbronville and put them in school they took advantage of it. They agreed to operate the recently constructed Viggo Hotel in exchange for board and room for their family. They leased Tipperary Farm and moved to the hotel. Mattie did the cooking. A Mrs. Longoria washed the dishes and did most of the cleaning in exchange for food for herself and her children. Ike kept the accounts and ordered supplies.

The hotel was the pride of Hebbronville. The owner, Viggo Köhler, had hired C. F. Luque to build it. It was constructed of poured concrete. People said it was indestructible. It towered over Hebbronville — it was three stories high. Mattie and Ike were still operating it when the girls returned from college in the spring of 1918.

Alleene had been teaching at La Partición, a ranch about thirty miles south of Hebbronville. She had three more months before her contract ran out, and she wanted to leave, so she asked Helen to finish out the term for her. School was held six months a year on the ranches. A teacher would teach six months on one ranch and then go to another ranch for six months. Helen had signed a contract to teach first and second grades in the Hebbronville public school, starting in September. To take the school at La Partición for three months worked out just right for her. She packed her belongings in a bundle that she tied behind her saddle and rode horseback from Hebbronville to La Partición.

She was engaged to Johnny, but she had not seen him for more than a year. She had corresponded with him while she was attending the university, but she had received no letters from him since she left there. Thinking he might have written to her at the address where the Sewells received mail during the last years they lived at Tipperary, she stopped by the Alta Vista Ranch on her way from Hebbronville to La Partición. And, to her surprise, there was a bag full of letters. They were addressed to her, from people at different places along a train route from Texas to New York. They told her a soldier on a troop train threw out her address and asked them to write to her. Now she knew Johnny was on his way overseas and that he was not allowed to say so but had devised this way of letting her know. And eventually she did hear directly from him.

Lee Norton was overseas, too — in the cavalry — and she was corresponding with him, more or less as a duty to the country's fighting men. When he wrote and proposed marriage, she said no as gently as she knew how.

CHAPTER SEVEN

None of the adults at La Partición spoke English, but that was no problem for Helen. She had studied Spanish in both high school and college and she spoke fluent Tex-Mex, as did everybody else in South Texas. She spoke Spanish in the ranch house but she taught in English. In Texas at that time teachers were not allowed to teach school in Spanish. It was even against the rules for students to speak Spanish on the schoolground in Hebbronville, although a class in Spanish was offered in the upper grades.

The school at La Partición was held in one room. The students ranged in age from six to fourteen.

The main ranch house was a huge, rambling rock building with a front porch. The foreman was a widower with a large family of girls. The two older girls were considered "old maids" and they were the housekeepers. They made Helen welcome and gave her a private room.

They served Mexican-style food, which Helen found quite enjoyable. But one day after they had killed and roasted a goat, she turned pale with nausea when one of the younger girls took a fork and reached in through the eye socket of the goat's head and pulled out some brains and ate them.

La Partición was an isolated place. There was no entertainment. Helen tried to fill the void by giving recitations of "Ginevra" and other readings. Even though most of the people did not understand English, they seemed to enjoy her performances.

Sometimes on Saturdays she painted their portraits, just to pass the time. She had learned something about portrait painting from a lady who lived in Alice, and had ordered art materials from Sears and Roebuck.

One Saturday Helen was sitting on the front porch, reading, when wives of some of the ranch hands started calling for her to come see something they had found beside the pila. Helen walked over. There lay a large coachwhip they had killed. It was still whipping its tail around. They assumed Helen would be afraid of the snake, and they pushed her toward it. She went along with the ploy, pretending to be frightened. Suddenly, she picked the snake up by its tail and started waving it around over her head, chasing the women. They screeched and screamed and scattered in every direction.

Helen was still at La Partición in July, when the primary election was held in Hebbronville. While she was in school at the university, she had developed a keen interest in the election process and the heated debates between the proponents of woman suffrage and some of the

Independence

men in government who believed that if women were given the vote the country would be ruined. And she was never more proud of being a Texan than when in March of 1918 the state legislature passed, and the governor signed, a bill giving women over twenty-one the right to vote in the primaries. Now, she couldn't bear the thought of not being there to cast her vote, so on election day she rode horseback the thirty miles to Hebbronville, voted, and rode back as far as Tipperary and spent the night. She had ridden forty-five miles that day. The next day she returned to La Partición.

There were a couple of parrots at the ranch. Every morning they would call out, "Don Pedro, vente por la casa para comer su comida" (Don Pedro, come to the house and get your breakfast). And they would sometimes sing a little song:

> Corre, corre, caballito, corre por favor,
> Y no deja el torito adelante, por favor.
> (Run, run little horse, run please,
> And don't let the little bull get ahead, please.)

The two parrots spoke only Spanish. They talked a lot about Don Pedro, but Helen was told it had been many years since he lived at the ranch.

At the end of three months Helen got on her horse and went back to Hebbronville. It was time to assume her duties as a teacher in the school there.

During the time she was away from home attending high school and college, Hebbronville had changed. Many people from south of the border had moved into the area to escape the political unrest and civil war in Mexico. The number of students enrolled in public school was dramatically larger. Helen had eighty students enrolled in the first and second grades. There were three or four Anglos and the rest were of Spanish descent. Most did not speak English. Helen knew the rule said she must conduct school in English. But nobody said she couldn't interpret and translate.

The schools Helen had been associated with on the ranches had no blackboards, but the school in Hebbronville was a new two-story brick building, and it had a blackboard in every room. She was delighted with hers and used it constantly. Each morning before her students arrived, she drew pictures on the board to help them learn English. They were apt. They learned fast. Soon everybody was speaking English. "Chil-

CHAPTER SEVEN

dren learn so easily from pictures." Years later education courses on college campuses would be stressing a new technique called visual aids.

J. Frank McGee was school superintendent. His wife and Miss Edna Pentecost taught the intermediate classes. There were only two students in high school. Mr. McGee taught them everything except Spanish — Helen taught them that.

Ike and Mattie were still operating the Viggo Hotel at that time, and all of the teachers lived there. Superintendent McGee and his wife lived in the bridal suite. "No brides ever came to that hotel, anyway." Helen waited tables and cleaned rooms in exchange for room and board, and to take some of the load off her mother.

On November 11 Hebbronville got news that the war was over. It came in over the telegraph lines at the depot. Helen had gone up to the roof of the three-story hotel to look out over Hebbronville and try to divide it into halves for the purpose of a Red Cross drive. While she was up there, Miss Pentecost called to her and told her the news. Helen came down the fire escape, three or four steps at a time, and she and Miss Pentecost went across the street to a little building that was being used as a church and climbed in through the window and rang the bell. "It was the only way we could think of to celebrate."

The influenza epidemic that devastated the United States after World War I hit Hebbronville that winter. The school superintendent had a bad case of it, with pneumonia. He became so ill that his wife felt they needed someone with them at night, so Helen volunteered. Soon Helen came down with the flu, and with pneumonia. There was a physician in Hebbronville at that time — a Dr. Stetson, who had come there in 1914 — and he attended Helen. But Mattie supplemented his care with her own time-tested treatment. She sent Harold out on the prairie to get a few roots of a plant called *yerba de la rabia* (hydrophobia weed) (*Acalypha radians* Torrey) that an old Mexican once introduced her to when Howard had typhoid fever. She believed it had cured Howard, and she had used it for fever ever since. She made a tea from the roots and poured as much of it down Helen as she could get her to take. When Helen recovered, Mattie was sure it was the root tea that cured her.

As Mattie grew older, hard work began to take its toll. Operating the hotel was getting to be too much for her, so Ike rented a house in Hebbronville and they and their children, including Helen, moved into it.

In March, 1919, County Judge A. M. Brumfield told Helen that

83

Independence

County/District Clerk W. A. Dannelly had announced his intention to resign. He said the court would have to appoint somebody to fill the position until the next election, and he wanted Helen to apply for it. She told him she wasn't interested: "I don't want to spend the rest of my life in Hebbronville."

Judge Brumfield said, "Why don't you talk it over with your parents?"

She did. They were eager for her to apply because they thought if she got the job it would keep her in Hebbronville. They told her, "Apply for it. You won't have to keep it forever—just till the next election." So she put her name in the pot.

The job paid sixty dollars a month—the same amount she was getting for teaching. But it would be a twelve-month-a-year job, while the teaching job paid only for the eight months school was in session. Also, the county/district clerk got paid extra for certain unofficial recording services.

Asa Draper was tax assessor at that time, and he sat in on the meeting of the county commissioners when they discussed the applications of Helen and the several men who had applied for the job. Somebody asked whether Helen knew how to use a typewriter. Asa said he would go over to the school and ask her. He did, and Helen said no.

He said, "Well, don't worry. I'll handle it."

He went back to the courthouse and told them, "You don't have to worry about her."

So Helen got the job. Asa brought her an old typewriter and a book on the touch system and said, "Here. Don't make a liar out of me." By the time she was sworn in she could type.

She wan't sure whether she was happy with the decision to leave teaching. It meant she would forfeit her opportunity to turn her provisional certificate into a permanent one. But the decision was made. She was now the county/district clerk of Jim Hogg County, with an office in the courthouse.

Within the next year two oil fields would be discovered in the Hebbronville area: O. W. Killam's Mirando City field, and J. W. Pippen's field at Randado. The recording of oil and gas leases gave Helen a lot of work. She also made abstracts of leases. And she made maps on linen for some of the oil men. Often these were services for which she was paid over and above her salary. What looked like big money rolled in.

She received plenty of advice about how best to invest her savings,

CHAPTER SEVEN

and some of the ranchers wanted to borrow money from her. She thought it over and decided to follow her own inclination. She decided to build herself a house. "I wanted something I could see." It cost her $2,000.

One of the oil companies sent a couple of men from Tulsa to try to talk her into acting as lease broker for them. She could do that, they said, in addition to her job at the courthouse. They made it sound appealing. The going price for a ten-year lease was one dollar per acre plus twenty-five cents rental. Her commission would probably amount to several times what her salary was. But she decided to turn it down. She wouldn't have felt comfortable. The people of the county were paying her to serve *them*. "But it was tempting."

The oil business was getting in Helen's blood. She was in a position to learn a great deal about it, and she did. She became remarkably knowledgeable, and she followed the oil and gas operations in Jim Hogg County with much interest from then on, often astonishing brokers and geologists with her acumen.

The brush was beginning to move into that area, and a few deer were coming in. Harold found a tiny fawn that seemed to be abandoned, and he brought it and gave it to Helen. She kept it with her constantly—at home at night, in the office during the day. As it grew, it became mischievous, and something of a nuisance. It nibbled the papers in the wastebasket at the office, even chewed on Helen's dresstail sometimes. But she loved that little deer.

One day a dog followed one of the oil men into the office, and when it saw the deer it began to bark. That frightened the deer and made it jump through the open window. Helen became hysterical. She was sure the deer would be killed—the window was high above the ground. She ran out and down the stairs and around to where the deer lay on the ground, and threw her arms around it, screaming: "He's dead. . . . He's dead. . . . Oh, he's dead. . . ."

As this was happening, a Texas Ranger rode up to the front of the courthouse. He tied his horse to the hitching post and walked over to see what all the screaming was about. By that time the deer had revived sufficiently to start nibbling on the leg of the man's trousers. Helen was still hysterical, still screaming, "He's dead."

The Ranger pulled his pants leg from the deer's mouth and remarked, "He seems pretty much alive to me, ma'm."

Helen looked up into the face of a tall slender man dressed neatly in khakis and a Stetson. It was her introduction to Pelton Bruce Har-

Independence

bison. He helped her to her feet and walked her and the deer to her office, and that was the last she saw of him for several weeks.

Hebbronville was a lonely, isolated place, with very few young people. But Helen had not had time to be lonely. She had been too involved with all the activity going on in connection with the oil business. Also, now the carpenters were working at building her house, and she spent every spare minute supervising that—she and her deer.

Johnny was back from the war, but she had not seen him. He had taken a job in a bank in Breckenridge, Texas. They corresponded, and they considered themselves engaged, but he had not said anything about setting a date for the wedding. Helen had remained faithful to him while he was in the Army, and since. She had not dated anybody else. She was sure she loved him.

There was a big picnic at Randado that summer, and Helen and Edna Pentecost went down there with Mr. and Mrs. McGee. Somebody had brought a set of dominoes, and Helen and Edna played Forty-two with Pelton Harbison and his friend Alec Reed. It was the first time Helen had seen the ranger since the day the deer jumped out the window.

Edna said later, "That Pell Harbison likes you, Helen."

"Well, I'm engaged to Johnny," Helen told her.

The following week Ranger Harbison showed up at Helen's office and asked whether she would come and interpret for a Spanish-speaking prisoner he wanted to take before the court. He explained that he spoke Spanish but that he was not allowed to interpret for his own prisoner. So Helen went with him to the court. After that, he came for her every time he brought in a Spanish-speaking prisoner.

Asa Draper seldom missed a thing that went on in Hebbronville, and he started kidding Helen about her new friend. She was not amused. She realized by this time that the ranger was shy, and she knew the men had been teasing him about his frequent visits to the courthouse. She told Asa to cut it out.

One day Asa told her if she wanted to run for election to the position she now held, she would have to get her name on the list that day; it was the last day it could be done. He said he had just come from Edds and Acklen Lumber Yard, and Henry Edds was down there in his office taking names of people who were going to run in the election, said if she was planning to run she'd better get down there and see Henry.

CHAPTER SEVEN

That this was the last day for declaring her intention to run for office both surprised and annoyed Helen. She was not pleased at the prospect of walking all the way down to the lumber yard, under the burning sun, through the deep sand (there were no sidewalks or paved streets in Hebbronville then). But she decided to do it — by now she liked being county/district clerk.

When she got to the lumber yard, all hot and sweaty, she learned that Asa had played a trick on her — it was not the last day to get her name on the ballot. The men all laughed at her. So when she started to walk back to the courthouse, she was not in the best of humor.

The Texas Rangers had a room at the lumber yard that they used as headquarters when they were in Hebbronville. As Helen walked out of the yard on her way back to the courthouse that day, she noticed Ranger Harbison walking in the same direction, only a few steps ahead of her. They walked on for a little while. Helen was annoyed at this, too. It must look pretty silly. He was bound to know she was there. She knew those men were back there laughing at them. She said, "Well, if you'll wait a minute, I'll walk with you." He waited. As they passed the drugstore, he invited her in for a dish of ice cream. She accepted.

Hebbronville permitted no secrets. Ranger Harbison — single and attractive — had up to now stayed cool and aloof, had shown no interest in any girl in Hebbronville. But now.... Was something going on between him and the county/district clerk?

Later that summer Mrs. William McMurrey, whose husband was at that time foreman at the Tom East ranch, invited Helen and Garland to spend a weekend at the ranch. They rode out Friday evening, getting there about dark.

It was destined to be an interesting weekend.

For one thing, as they sat around talking that evening, the McMurreys described for them the time a few years back when Pancho Villa's men raided the ranch. Helen and Garland had known about the raid, of course — everybody in that area knew about it. It had been gory. The Texas Rangers had been tipped off and had surprised the bandits in the middle of the raid. No Ranger was lost, but several of the bandits were killed. The girls had heard the tales. They had even seen photographs of the dead bodies lying around. Their brother Harold was one of the young men who helped the Rangers bring the bandits' saddles and guns to Hebbronville. Tonight, the girls relived what they already

Independence

knew and learned more details. It was fresh in their minds when they went to bed in an isolated room at the back of the house. Garland examined the door and said, "There's no way to lock this."

Helen said, "Why do we need to lock the door?"

"Well, in case bandits come or something."

"Oh, Garland!"

"Well, what if they did?"

Helen, exasperated, shoved a dresser against the door and got into bed.

About three o'clock the next morning the girls were awakened by the sound of the dresser scraping across the floor. Somebody was pushing the door open. They both sat straight up. Helen didn't even attempt to conceal her fear.

But it was only Mrs. McMurrey coming to call them to breakfast. She cooked breakfast for the ranch hands at that time every morning, so they could catch their horses and start working the cattle before it got too hot. She got the girls up for breakfast with the hands.

Later that day Mrs. McMurrey invited them to go with her to take a cake and some cold drinks out to a pila where a bunch of Texas Rangers were camped. The Rangers often camped out on the ranches for days or weeks at a time, cutting for sign (looking for trails of bandits). Ranchers liked to have Rangers on their land, as this discouraged the bandits. It was Captain Wright and some of his men who camped on the East ranch then, and Pell Harbison was among them. Mrs. McMurrey may or may not have been in league with the busybodies of Hebbronville, but she invited all the Rangers to come to the ranch house for dinner that night. There was that Ranger, crossing Helen's path again.

And he began stopping by her office when he was in Hebbronville, just to chat. At first he tied his horse in front of the courthouse, where he was accustomed to tie it. But the men teased him about hanging around the courthouse, and he started tying the horse behind the jail so his visits would not be so obvious. As far as Helen was concerned, she liked him well enough but she was in love with Johnny.

Helen was living with her parents in Hebbronville that summer. One Sunday afternoon she was across the street visiting with Evelyn Briscoe, whose husband, Payne, was president of the Hebbronville bank. They were engaged in a popular local pastime—playing the Victrola. Garland came and said Pell Harbison and Alec Reed had come to invite

CHAPTER SEVEN

Garland and Helen to go for a ride with them in Alec's car. Helen said, "No, I better not. I'm engaged to Johnny."

Mrs. Briscoe: "Why don't you go? Johnny's not here, and you never get to go anyplace."

Helen decided to go.

They rode out to a place called the Trap, about two or three miles out of town. It was owned by Alec's father and was one of those places used for holding cattle until they could be fed and watered before being driven on to the shipping pens. Alec drove the car, and on the way out and back Pell entertained the girls by shooting jack rabbits with his forty-five revolver. When they got back to town, they took the girls to the cafe and ordered coffee. Helen and Garland didn't drink coffee at that time. They sat, ill at ease, for a little while; then they went outside and walked up and down in front of the cafe until the men finished their coffee and came out. So much for Helen's first date with Pell.

He continued to come by her office to chat, and one day he brought an album of photographs that he wanted to show her. They were pictures of him and his friends, some of them girl friends, taken when he had lived in Goliad, Texas. And he started coming by the Sewells' house when he'd be in town, and he and Helen would play the Victrola. Alleene had given Ike a Victrola for Christmas, and Helen ordered popular records once each month, from Thomas A. Goggan, San Antonio. She kept the ones she liked and sent the others back. Her collection included "It's a Long, Long Way to Tipperary," "Till We Meet Again," "Over There," "When Johnny Comes Marching Home," "The Rose of Normandy," "My Wild Irish Rose," "Red River Valley."

One day Pell came to Helen's office and said, "Well, I've heard many interesting things today, but the most interesting of all was when I learned Miss Helen Sewell was mortgaged." How it could have taken him that long to discover she was supposed to be engaged is puzzling, especially given Hebbronville's proclivity for news dissemination.

In a few days Pell dropped by with another photo album and showed Helen a picture of a girl in Goliad with whom he was corresponding. Her name was Maud. He and Helen continued to listen to Victrola records in her parents' living room. He nicknamed her "Skeeter," and he started asking her to give up Johnny for him. By this time everybody in town knew Pell was in love with the feisty little county/district clerk. And they were dating regularly. But she corresponded with Johnny and still considered herself engaged to him.

Independence

That Helen and Pell were drifting closer and closer together was obvious. But their relationship was not destined to be a smooth one. One evening when a carnival was in town he told her he did not feel well enough to take her to the carnival, that he was sick. She decided to go, anyway, with her brother Harold. Ike had a model-T Ford by that time, and Helen drove it to the carnival and parked beside Mrs. Briscoe, who was sitting in her car. They chatted and watched the people milling around. Larry Hall, a handsome Ranger and one of Pell's colleagues, came and asked Helen, "Where's Pell?"

She said, "He's not doing so well tonight."

Larry guffawed and said, "You can say that again!" And he walked off laughing. Helen began to have a feeling he knew something she didn't.

Then Mrs. Briscoe said, "Don't look now, but you need to see who just drove up in the car behind me."

There was George Edds with the sister of Larry Hall's girl friend in the front seat, and on the back seat, none other than Larry's girl friend herself and Pell Harbison! The girl's hair was loose and hanging down over her shoulders. Indeed she was beautiful. Helen had never worn her hair down like that when she was out in public. She considered it immodest.

When Pell apologized to Helen, making excuses, she told him, "I'm not telling you who to go with, but you're not going with that girl and me at the same time." And she turned and walked away.

The next day Captain Wright took Pell and the other rangers and went to Galveston to help put down some trouble.

After Helen had time to think about it, she knew she should not really be surprised if Pell showed up with another girl sometimes. She was still corresponding with Johnny, still considered herself engaged to him, still refused to tell Pell she would give Johnny up. Besides, every girl in town was after Pell. One of them was always telling Helen about compliments Pell paid her when he'd see her in the post office. Helen thought maybe she wouldn't have been so angry if that girl had not had her beautiful hair hanging down. Besides, he lied to her!

Then the trouble in Galveston was over and the rangers were back in Hebbronville, and there was Pell in the post office, opening his mail box, when Helen walked in. She noticed he was having trouble with the box. When he turned to face her, he looked ill. He asked whether he could come to the house that evening and talk things over. She weak-

CHAPTER SEVEN

ened and said yes. When he arrived, he had the biggest box of chocolates he could find, and when he left the spat was over. But every time she thought about that girl and Pell riding all over town in the back seat of that car, she burned.

So it probably was with a certain amount of hidden—or not so hidden—glee that she told Pell she had a letter from Johnny and that he was coming to see her.

The next day Pell and the other Rangers left town and stayed gone all the time Johnny was visiting Helen. The men around town teased Pell about that, too. The tall silent ranger was losing some of his invulnerability.

CHAPTER EIGHT

While Johnny was in Hebbronville, he and Helen played records until they wore out the Victrola needles, and he told her he'd buy her some in Laredo when he changed trains. After he was gone, a small package showed up at the post office, and the postmaster thought it might contain an engagement ring. Word got around town that Helen had decided in favor of that curly-headed ex-soldier. Helen found the gossip amusing. Even Pell seemed to enjoy the joke. Actually, Johnny had not said anything about setting a date for a wedding.

Helen's little deer was growing up, but it still tried to stay right at her heels. It went with her to work. It followed her when she went to the post office, or to anyplace else in town. At night it stayed in the Sewells' yard, was always waiting for her in the mornings. But it was becoming something of a problem — it ate Mattie's rose bushes and other plants. Then, one day it pawed a little boy. Mattie said the deer had to go. And Helen knew her mother was right. She took it down to the Thompsons' place and turned it into a field behind the house, where they had several other deer. She went down there every evening to visit with it and feed it pecans. But the little deer did not live. Some people said it died of a broken heart.

In September, 1919, Helen went up to Alice for a weekend. She went by train, on Saturday the thirteenth. The day was beautiful, with a temperature already slightly cooler than in summer. Mrs. Presnall gave a dinner party for her, and they spent most of the evening playing the Victrola and dancing. Johnny was in Alice that weekend, and he and Helen were having fun.

In the middle of the merry-making Mr. Presnall announced that he wanted everybody to leave the house immediately and go to the bank. He had been watching the weather while the others were enjoying the party, and he believed they were in a pre-hurricane condition. He said

CHAPTER EIGHT

the new bank building was much sturdier than the house, so they would be better off there.

The winds were strong and the rain started coming down in sheets. Some of the younger men, including the Presnalls' son Homer, worked most of the night bringing people to the shelter of the bank. It got crowded.

At one time Johnny and Helen stood by the heavy glass window at the front of the bank and put their hands against the glass, feeling it give from the force of the wind. Mr. Presnall told them to get away from there: "That window is liable to break and kill both of you!"

One young woman had a miscarriage in the back room of the bank that night, with Mrs. Presnall in attendance.

After a while the wind stopped and everything got very still. Nobody went home. These people knew what a hurricane was. They knew the calm meant the eye was passing over them, that in a few minutes the winds would come at them as strong as ever, from the opposite direction.

The storm didn't do a lot of damage in Alice—uprooted a few trees, blew away some porches. It was not until the next afternoon that they learned it had practically destroyed Corpus Christi, only forty miles away.

When Helen finally got back to Hebbronville, Pell said she should have stayed home in the first place.

In 1919 J. Frank Dobie was just getting started on his writing career. He was in Hebbronville one day to make a talk. Helen later recalled: "I don't remember what organization invited him. But he gave the talk at the courthouse—where all community meetings were held in those days, even church services."

Mr. Dobie had a folk poem that he wanted young Alfred Draper to read, but Myrtle refused to allow Alfred to read it because it contained the word *hell*.

Helen volunteered to read the poem. "I guess I shocked a few people. But I read it—I felt sorry for Mr. Dobie when Myrtle acted that way."

Pell continued to ask Helen to give up Johnny for him, and she continued to hesitate. One day when they were standing side by side pulling mail from their boxes at the post office, they noticed that Pell had a letter from Maud and Helen had one from Johnny. Pell said, "Let's trade letters. I'll let you read Maud's if you'll let me read Johnny's."

Independence

Helen's conscience told her such behavior stopped short of being honorable. But she did agree to it. "I was curious."

If either of them was hoping to learn secrets, he or she was disappointed. The letters were remarkably alike. In essence what they said was "You seem to have changed."

Pell's handsome colleague Larry Hall happened to ride by the Sewell house one weekend when Helen was out in the yard painting a portrait of a little neighbor girl. He stopped and admired the painting, and asked whether she would paint a picture of him.

When Pell learned Larry was sitting for Helen to paint his portrait, he immediately requested that she paint one of him. And she did.

Helen knew everybody in Hebbronville was pulling for Pell in the triangle of Pell, Johnny, and Helen. Tena Draper told her one day, "I don't see why you hang onto that boy Johnny, when Pell is such a wonderful person." Helen didn't let it worry her. She went merrily along. Fiesta was coming up, and that was no time to be burdened with decisions.

Each September, after the crops were harvested and the cattle sold, Fiesta was held in the Hebbronville plaza across from the Catholic church. Vendors built little wooden structures, or booths, all around the edge of the plaza. Here they displayed various kinds of wares: costume jewelry, fancy combs for women's hair, belts and other small leather goods, and all kinds of trinkets. There were booths selling cooked cabrito, hot tamales, tortillas, coffee, and pop. Also, in the early days there were gambling booths at Fiesta.

Music from the plaza drifted over the town and put everybody in a festive mood. It was provided by bands composed of local talent. In the evenings, the young people promenaded in the center of the plaza, the boys walking in a circle in one direction, the girls walking in the opposite direction.

Fiesta was a magical time. It was a time to abandon cares, to look for adventure, to sparkle. And into this expanse of merriment in one of the earlier years rode a black-clad horseman waving his revolver over his head and shooting into the air. Screams of "Pancho Villa!!!" came from all sides as men, women, and children scattered in every direction.

There was no reason to doubt that this was Pancho Villa. The famous bandit and his men had been raiding ranches in the area all that summer. And the man on the horse fit the bandit's description. But it turned out to be a prank. The horseman was a local cowboy dis-

CHAPTER EIGHT

guised as Pancho Villa. Oscar Thompson was the sheriff then, and he arrested the masquerader and fined him. The cowboy is said to have declared that the fun was worth what it cost him.

One day shortly after the 1920 Fiesta was over, Helen was at the depot seeing Pell off to Laredo. She suddenly, on impulse, turned to him and said, "I'm going to marry you." She couldn't have said why she did it at that particular moment.

Pell didn't touch her. He didn't even move toward her. He just looked at her with a twinkle in those dark eyes and said, "I knew it all the time."

Later, Garland said, "You mean he didn't even hold your hand?"

"No."

"Did it make you mad when he said he already knew?"

"He probably did know! Him and his self-confidence!"

That night Helen wrote several letters to Johnny and tore them up before she finally did one she was more or less satisfied with. The next morning she took it to the post office and mailed it.

The incoming mail that day brought a letter from Johnny. It asked her to set a date for their wedding.

Garland said, "How did it make you feel?"

"Awfully sorry for Johnny."

"Are you sorry you decided to marry Pell?"

"No."

When Pell returned from Laredo, he brought her a diamond lavaliere, as a token of their understanding. He said he'd get her an engagement ring soon.

On November 11 a big celebration was held in Hebbronville. One of the attractions was a pilot with a little rickety plane, offering rides for $10 each. He said the first two to sign up could go for $7.50. Helen and Garland signed. Other people signed up also, among them George Edds and the E. L. Armstrongs' daughter Florence. A lot of people gathered to see them off. In the crowd was Mattie Sewell, who was distressed that her daughters were going up in that thing.

Helen went first. The passenger seat was not enclosed, and when she put out her hand to wave to her audience the wind whipped her arm around as if it were a rag. There was so much noise she couldn't hear a word the pilot was saying. He flew over the town and out past Mesquite Creek. It wasn't all that much of an adventure.

When the plane landed, Helen climbed out and Garland climbed

Independence

in. Helen turned around and there stood Mattie and Pell. He looked even more annoyed than Mattie. He said, "I'm not sure I want to marry somebody who is foolish enough to go up in that flimsy contraption."

When Helen told Garland about it later, Garland said, "What did you say?"

"Nothing. Wasn't anything *to* say. It was done then."

"You didn't say, 'Well, just don't marry me, then'?"

"No."

Pell was in Laredo for a few days that winter, and while he was gone Helen did something that displeased him—she accepted a box of candy from one of the oil men. It was all very innocent. The man was looking for land to lease. Helen knew Mrs. Henry Yaeger had some land she wanted to lease, so she sent the man to see Mrs. Yaeger, and to show his appreciation he bought Helen a box of chocolates. By the time Pell got back to town the candy was all gone. But he heard about it. Some of those men in Hebbronville were always looking for something to have fun with—they probably made a good story out of it. Pell went to her office and said, "Could I have a piece of that candy you're hiding?"

"I don't have any candy," Helen told him.

Pell shot back, "I know you do."

"No. I don't."

He said, "Well. I brought you something from Laredo, but I guess I won't give it to you, now that you are lying to me."

She said, "I'm not lying. I'm telling you the truth. I don't have any candy." Then she added, mischievously, "I ate it all up."

What he had brought her was a beautiful wool scarf that was gray with red stripes and had fringe. He did finally give it to her, after the spat was over.

In February, 1921, there was to be a celebration in Laredo, in honor of George Washington's birthday. Pell was asked to lead the parade, riding his fine horse. Mrs. E. L. Armstrong and her father, H. C. Yaeger, planned to drive over for the occasion in Mr. Yaeger's car, and they invited Helen to go with them.

Lots of people from Hebbronville went to Laredo that day to see their favorite ranger lead the parade. People lined the streets. Helen and Evelyn Briscoe, Jewell Wallace and her little sister Joanne, George Edds, and several other friends were standing on the corner by the Hamilton Hotel.

CHAPTER EIGHT

There came Pell on that beautiful horse, sitting regally in his fine saddle, at the head of the parade, leading the Texas Rangers and other notables. When he got to the hotel, he dismounted and, leading his horse, walked over to where Helen stood and handed her a small package saying, "Here are your Victrola needles." Then he got back on his horse and the parade continued.

Helen was amused by the joke about the Victrola needles, remembering how a package of Victrola needles had been mistaken for an engagement ring by people in Hebbronville after Johnny had visited her. She smiled at Pell's sense of humor as she walked around the corner to open the little package, feeling sure she knew what she would find inside. Joanne followed her, and when she saw the big diamond Helen was slipping on her finger she exclaimed: "My! Doesn't it shine!"

All the rest of that day people kept kidding Helen about being important enough to stop a parade. And then they'd say, "My, doesn't it shine?"

Now, the ranger and the county/district clerk were formally engaged. Helen made a few trips by train to Laredo to shop at the August C. Richter Company for wedding clothes, and she finally bought everything she needed except shoes. She couldn't find any white shoes that fit her long narrow feet. She wasn't concerned. They had not set a date for the wedding. She thought she had plenty of time.

She did write to the secretary of state in Austin to ask whether she could issue her own marriage license. He wrote back: "Yes. If you didn't, who would? You are the only one there who has the authority."

Before she had occasion to issue her own, however, she was called upon to issue an important marriage license for somebody else—in June, 1921, Garland married Leuin David. He was one of the sons of the W. W. Davids the Sewells had met at the big Fourth of July picnic on the McCampbell ranch in 1909. At the time he and Garland married, Leuin and his brother owned a water-well drilling business in Jim Hogg County. Leuin and Garland established a home in Hebbronville and lived there for many years.

Helen's interest in creative writing had stayed with her through the years, surfacing every now and then in the form of poetry. She had written mostly for her own pleasure and had not tried to publish anything. But in the spring of 1921 she submitted the following poem to *Alcalde*, the University of Texas alumni magazine, and it came out in the May issue.

Independence

RANCH FEVER
(after John Masefield)

I must go back to the ranch again
    To the lonely ranch and ride—
And all I ask is a pony game
    And a six-shooter by my side.

I must go back where the bandits raid
    And the lonely coyotes howl,
Where the cactus grows, and the buzzards parade,
    To the home of the prairie owl.

I shall perch myself on a sandhill high
    And look in the distant haze;
No doubt I'll smile and heave a sigh
    As I think of my Varsity days.
                —Helen Marie Sewell

    In August, Helen took a few days of vacation and went to visit the Presnalls in Alice, and while she was there Pat Craighead, who was sheriff of Jim Hogg County, died. Helen received a telegram that said: "Come home immediately. Need to hold commissioners court. P. B. Harbison to be appointed sheriff."

    She took the next train from Alice to Hebbronville, and on her twenty-fifth birthday—August 19, 1921—Pelton Bruce Harbison, at age thirty-five, was sworn in as sheriff of Jim Hogg County.

    The following poem surfaced in Hebbronville about that time, describing the area and its new law enforcement officer. It is attributed to Mrs. Jack Miles.

Just where I am, no body knows—
I am in a land where the mescal flows,
Where the centipede crawls, and the coyotes howl
When the moon doesn't shine, the Bootleggers prowl
Where Tequilla is peddled on burros back—
And the Rangers are hot, right on their track.

The bottles they captured, I cannot tell
But they captured enough to fill up a well
They poured it in, and set it a fire
If Steve Murphy knew that, it would sure raise his ire.
These seven brave Rangers did not seem to care
For they destroyed the tequilla, mescal and beer.

CHAPTER EIGHT

The sand is so deep a person can't walk
And to pull through it makes a little Ford talk.
Henry and Lizzie go hand in hand
They sure pull together when they hit the sand.
There are thorns on the cacti and thorns on the trees
Horns on the snakes and sand full of fleas.

The lizzards and tarantulas are thick in the land
Every thing down here is an enemy to man.
Even the water is hard as a rock
To drink it very long would sure stop your clock.
Wash your face lightly, cannot rub it in.

It gets so hot in summer, the corn pops in the field
They plant their summer gardens, it is winter before they yield
They have roasting-ears for Christmas, picking cotton, cutting cane.
It's a "land of wonders" for it never rains.
The frijoles keep on growing, also black-eyed peas
The folks don't worry, they take life with ease.

The Sheriff with his six-shooter dangling by his side
Is trying his very best to win himself a bride—
A black haired little lassie with eyes so big and blue.
If I'm a judge of nature I judge that she'll be true.
He rides a spotted pony, his given name is Pell
When he goes after law breakers, you bet he gives them Hell.

With Pell

CHAPTER NINE

Newly appointed Sheriff Harbison moved into the apartment furnished for him at the jail and set about bringing eight-year-old Jim Hogg County under his control. He would enforce the law of course. But he didn't plan to stop there—he had his own thoughts about what was good for a community and he intended to be guided by them. He didn't expect any trouble. A sheriff in South Texas in 1921 managed his county with pretty much of a free hand.

One of the first things he did was to start meeting the two incoming trains each day, and if a woman he believed to be a prostitute got off he put her right back on the train. He told Helen, "They're heading for the oil fields, and it's hard enough to keep order there without the addition of loose women."

Helen wanted to know how he knew they were loose women. "He just laughed."

Another thing he did was to declare an evening curfew—all children were to be in their houses by nine o'clock. His favorite horse at that time was a beautiful paint, and he began riding it up and down the streets about eight-thirty, often trading jokes and witticisms with the children. They called him Mr. Pell. He was their hero.

He was liked and respected by the adults of the community also, in spite of his strict ways. Sometimes he even had to arbitrate domestic quarrels, and one thing he didn't tolerate was physical violence against women. He once told a man, "Wife beating may be common practice on the other side of the border, but I better not catch you at it in Jim Hogg County."

His reputation for being fearless and authoritative was well established around Hebbronville even before he became sheriff. He had dark brown eyes that some people said could burn a hole through a person when Pell willed it. He lived by a code of honor all his own. Larry Hall said he had more than once seen Pell ride up and jerk a fleeing

Mexican outlaw from his horse when other Rangers would have shot the fellow.

This shy, sensitive man Helen had promised to marry evidently had guts of steel. He also had winning ways, especially where the ladies were concerned. In 1921 the women on the committee to decorate the community Christmas tree declared they couldn't get along without his help, and they cajoled him into spending all of Christmas Eve afternoon putting up the tree and helping decorate it.

For several years it had been customary to have a Christmas tree in the courthouse, and to assemble there for a community party on Christmas Eve. It was an important affair that had started out as an entertainment for school children but had spread to encompass the whole community. All the public school children came, with their parents and brothers and sisters. Most of the leading citizens and their families came. Gifts for friends as well as for the needy were piled under the tree. Mrs. Oscar Thompson often spent weeks before Christmas at her sewing machine, making clothes for children of some of the poorer families. Everybody contributed to the mountain of wrapped presents, and nobody went home empty-handed.

While Pell was helping the ladies with the Christmas tree, Helen was driving her father's model-T touring car around town, picking up gifts and bringing them to the courthouse. On one of the trips she stopped to admire the tree. It was a beautiful fir, maybe eight feet tall. It had been shipped from one of the northern states to Laredo and had come from there on the Tex-Mex train—just as Helen and her family had done almost thirteen years ago. She remembered that first Christmas in Texas—with the little sugarberry bush for a tree and homemade teddy bears for gifts. What a difference thirteen years could make! Nobody used sugarberry bushes for Christmas trees any more; everybody bought shipped-in fir. She stood and watched as the ladies wrapped the big tree in tinsel and cranberry and popcorn garlands, and Pell placed an angel on the very top.

At last the tree was decorated and all the packages were stashed under it, and everybody went home to eat and get dressed for the party that was to start to seven o'clock. Pell and Helen were the last to leave the courthouse. He told her that the women had been teasing him all afternoon, trying to find out when he and Helen were planning to be married. He said, "Skeeter, they think they're so smart! They're sure

CHAPTER NINE

Helen and Pell in serapes and sombreros.

With Pell

Helen and Pell on sand dune near Hebbronville. Edith Miller, secretary at Edds Lumber Yard in background.

CHAPTER NINE

Pell and Helen, shortly after they were married.

With Pell

Pell and Helen, on steps of the house Helen already owned, shortly after they were married. *Below:* Mattie and Ike Sewell, probably at the Harbison ranch before Pell and Helen moved to Austin.

CHAPTER NINE

Seven-month-old Hazel with her hand in the fishbowl. This is the photo that won Helen $100 in a national contest sponsored by Kodak and Fox Studios. *Below:* The poured-concrete house Pell and Helen built on their ranch in 1928.

With Pell

Ten-year-old Reginald in foreground, spreading chopped cane in the trench silo. Field hands operating the ensilage cutter. Pell at edge of silo, on left.

CHAPTER NINE

we're going to get married tomorrow. Why don't we get married tonight, before the party, and surprise them?"

Well. That was a surprising suggestion, all right.

Here she was, all disheveled and dirty from running around in an open car, tramping in and out in the sand, up and down the steps with all those packages.

But Helen liked surprises. And the thought of putting something over on the busybodies appealed to her. She said, "Why not?"

It was nearly five o'clock. They had to be back at the courthouse at seven. That didn't leave a lot of time to plan and execute a wedding. They knew there was no Protestant minister in town. But Judge Brumfield was at home, and he sometimes married people.

Pell went to make arrangements with the judge. Helen went to tell her mother to have a wedding dinner ready in one hour.

Then Helen started to bathe and dress. When she was ready to get into her new white dress, she remembered she had no white shoes. She had a new pair of black satin shoes, but she thought they'd look absurd with that filmy white dress. She put on her black shoes and reached for a new black satin dress Alleene had made for her. She had always heard it was bad luck to be married in black. But she didn't have time to be concerned about that now.

Somehow, they got through the wedding and the dinner. They barely made it to the courthouse in time for the party. Pell said, "Let's don't tell anybody." But evidently he couldn't keep it. The very first thing he did when they got there was walk up to Mr. and Mrs. McGee and say, "Guess what. Skeeter and I got married awhile ago."

Everybody had been outwitted, and Helen and Pell felt very smug about it.

During the evening Pell learned that Asa Draper and some of the others were planning to manhandle him and lock him in his own jail after the party was over, and keep him there all night. He told Helen he would have to sneak away before the party ended. She was not to worry. He would be back—sometime. It would be easier for her if she didn't know where he was going.

So on her wedding night Helen went to her parents' home, packed a few clothes, and waited.

Her own house had been built for some time, and she had bought a bit of furniture—a bed and a few pieces for the living room—but she hadn't yet bought anything for the kitchen. Bathroom fixtures had

With Pell

been installed but there was no water supply. She had supposed they'd have plenty of time to get the house ready to live in before they married. But, now. . . . Oh well, she wouldn't worry about it.

Shortly after midnight Pell showed up, and they walked to their new home. He told her he had been at the Catholic school where they were having a dance. He had promised them some time ago that he'd attend, to make sure order was maintained. He had momentarily forgotten about his promise, but had remembered it while at the Christmas party and had decided to combine duty with strategy in evading Asa and the others who planned to play a prank on him. He figured Asa wouldn't think to look for him at the Catholic school. And he hadn't.

The Catholic organization in Hebbronville had in 1897 established a school called Colegio Altamirano, where students were taught in Spanish. It was this school that was holding the dance on Helen's wedding night.

On Christmas morning there not only was no cookstove at the Harbison honeymoon house, there was no food except a cake Pell had received as a Christmas present. He said, "Who ever heard of cake for breakfast? And no coffee!" Helen didn't drink coffee, anyway. It didn't bother her. Pell finally went and begged a cup of coffee from his new mother-in-law.

It was not Helen's fault that she was not able to serve her husband a proper breakfast that first day. But she really didn't anticipate being a perfect housekeeper, anytime. She didn't like to keep house. She preferred to work in the office, or even in the field. But she *would* keep house, of course, because it was something that was expected of every woman.

Hebbronville at that time had no power plant, no water or sewer system. Helen and Pell—like other families who had no well of their own—bought water by the barrel from a man who went around with a donkey cart. They used an outside toilet (called a *casita* in that area), and their lights were oil lamps.

A couple of weeks after they were married, Pell had to go to Laredo for a meeting and Helen went to the depot to see him off. When he was ready to board the train, instead of kissing her or hugging her, he shook hands with her. If she wanted to kick him, it wasn't the first time she'd had that urge, nor would it be the last.

Pell had always cooperated with the Customs officers. He had good

CHAPTER NINE

friends in the organization. Now that he no longer needed the apartment in the jail for himself, he offered it as living quarters for these men when they were in Hebbronville. Some of them, and some of the Texas Rangers, were often at the Harbisons' house in the evenings, drinking coffee, smoking cigarettes, and talking. At that time, the different law enforcement groups were to a great extent involved in the same thing—keeping alcoholic beverages from being smuggled from Mexico into the United States.

When the Eighteenth Amendment to the U.S. Constitution became effective January 16, 1920, it initiated large-scale smuggling of tequila and mescal (two Mexican liquors made from the agave plant). Most of the smugglers were Mexicans, many of them the same men who had raided Texas border ranches with Pancho Villa a few years before. Texas law enforcement officers referred to them as *mescaleros,* or *tequileros.* They moved the contraband across the essentially uninhabited prairies of the border counties, with San Diego in Duval County an important point of rendezvous. They usually moved it by pack train, through the brush, but now and then one would become brave enough to try the roads, in an old truck. That was not very practical, however, because even where there were roads it was difficult to get a truck through the sand in dry weather, or the mud in wet.

Talk around the coffee table at the Harbison house was almost always about how the officers had either won or lost a battle with the smugglers, and about strategy and technique, and it was always spiced with interesting vernacular. The officers patrolled on horseback and carried revolvers and rifles. The smugglers called them *rinches,* or *empleados,* and of course they hated them.

The Texas Rangers spent a lot of time camping out on ranches, cutting for sign of trails of the smugglers. And when they found a pack train of contraband, they often had a battle on their hands. They'd tell how they flushed a band of *mescaleros* out of a *mogote* (a thick patch of brush) and induced them to "give down their milk" (cooperate, talk). If one tried to run away, they "naturalized" him (shot him).

Once, when one of the Rangers felt his position was insecure, Captain Will Wright told him to "just sit in the boat" (be patient).

If the officers came upon a shipment of illegal goods, they broke any bottles of liquor and confiscated the equipment and kept it until they had enough to warrant holding a sale, and then they auctioned it off.

With Pell

The Nueces Strip, where law and order had been hard to hold onto ever since Texas took that territory from Mexico, was still a place where law enforcement officers earned their pay.

Soon after Helen and Pell married, he had a well drilled, bought a windmill, and had a septic tank dug. They had hot and cold running water in their bathroom and kitchen, and plenty of water for outside watering. Helen was in heaven. She had always wanted trees and flowers. Now she could have them.

One time after John Nance Garner had been electioneering in Hebbronville, he sent Helen a package of flower seeds. She planted them in a box in her office window, and saved seeds from them and kept replanting them, so that she had flowers in that window box most of the time. Now that she had plenty of water at her house, she used some seeds from those flowers to plant herself a flower garden by the house. She also planted a couple of fig trees. "I had been so hungry for flowers and trees."

Another thing Pell did right away after they were married was to have a storm cellar dug in their yard. When he was a boy in Goliad, he had lived through a tornado (May 18, 1902) that killed his mother and a brother and sister, and he had been phobic about storms ever since. Few people in Hebbronville had storm cellars. But the Harbisons did.

Elections were coming up, and Helen and Pell needed a car to electioneer in. He bought the first car with glass windows in Hebbronville. It was a model-T Ford coupe. It was fancy, with plush upholstery and a vase for flowers. Needless to say, Helen kept the vase filled with fresh-cut arrangements. The car had been more or less forced on the local dealer, D. D. David, by the Ford Motor Company, and had been in the showroom for several months. Nobody wanted to buy it. They said it was top-heavy. But Helen and Pell luxuriated in it without problems as they drove around counting votes.

Pell didn't know how to drive a car, so Helen taught him. It went all right except for Pell's language. She knew he cussed. She had heard him cuss sometimes. He never cussed people, and he tried not to cuss too much around women and girls. But cussing came as naturally to him as breathing, and when he was frustrated he cussed no matter who was there. Helen had never seen him as frustrated as he was when he was trying to learn to drive that car. It was "Dammit!" and "God-dammit!" and "God-dammit to hell!" plus a few less genteel expres-

CHAPTER NINE

sions, every time he couldn't get the car to do what he wanted it to. But he eventually began to get the hang of it, and the car became more cooperative.

Helen and Pell both won in the election, and they settled comfortably into their positions for two more years. All went well. The sheriff was in command. In fact, he found it easier to control the town and county than that stubborn model-T, or the young lady who was so at home in its driver's seat.

As they were finishing lunch one day, Captain Will Wright of the Texas Rangers came by their house looking for Pell. He sat at the table with them to have a cup of coffee. He seemed preoccupied. Pell said, "Something on your mind?"

"Yes. I want you to go to an adjoining county and arrest the sheriff's father."

Pell didn't say anything. He just sat and looked at the captain. Helen sucked in her breath and concentrated on keeping her mouth shut. She knew Pell would be furious if she butted in. Finally Pell asked, "What's the charge?"

Captain Wright said, "Cattle theft." And he handed Pell a warrant for the man's arrest.

Pell didn't have a regular deputy, so he tried to deputize somebody just for that day, but he couldn't find anybody in Hebbronville who was willing to help him with the mission he was about to undertake. They all said it couldn't be done—no man could go over there and arrest that sheriff's father. Pell got in his car and started out, alone.

Helen was not working at the courthouse then. She was pregnant with their first child, and she had resigned her position as county/district clerk. After Pell left that day, she went out in her flower garden and hoed all the plants, even those she had hoed the day before. She couldn't remember being this worried about anything in her whole life. She knew Captain Wright had the authority to order Pell to do what he had asked him to do. And she knew Pell would do it, or die trying. And he just might die—those people over there had a reputation for ignoring the law. They were dangerous. She told her plants, "He doesn't have enough sense to be afraid!"

When around four o'clock Pell drove up to the courthouse with his prisoner and another man in the car, Helen wasn't the only person in Hebbronville who breathed easier. The whole town had been on edge ever since he left.

With Pell

That night Pell told Helen about the arrest. He said that when he got to the other town, he noticed lots of people standing around on the streets. He said to himself, "Well, they've been tipped off—they're expecting me." He found the sheriff and his father and several other men at the cafe. They were all wearing revolvers. When Pell announced that the man was under arrest, the sheriff stood up and said, "Nobody arrests my father."

Pell said, "I have orders to take him to Hebbronville for questioning."

Helen could imagine the in-command look that accompanied those words. She said, "Then what happened?"

"I just reasoned with them. They were afraid the man was gonna get hurt. I convinced them I'd protect him, and I suggested that his son come along to make sure."

Helen said, "So that explains why you came back with two men instead of one?"

Pell said, "Uh-huh." And that was the end of the discussion.

In June, 1923, Helen and Pell bought one thousand acres of undeveloped land, about seven miles south of Hebbronville and only about three miles from the E. L. Armstrongs' El Sordo Ranch. They did it on the spur of the moment, as they did many other things. And they were very pleased with themselves. The brush had not yet moved onto this land; it was covered with tall grass. They would drive down sandy Randado Road in the evenings after work and look across their rolling acres of waving grass, and plan. They expected their baby in November. This ranch would be a perfect place to bring up a family.

They paid cash for their land. Pell had worked as a barber in Goliad before he became a Texas Ranger. He had worked long hours and saved his money until he had enough to set up his own elaborate barbershop, and he had invested in a farm in Goliad County. He owned the farm, plus a $7,500 savings account that resulted from the sale of his barbershop. Helen had saved $2,500. Together, they had enough to buy the thousand acres.

Hebbronville still celebrated with Fiesta in the fall, and it was still a time of enchantment and felicity, but gambling was no longer part of it. Pell thought that was not good for the community. The people elected him, and he believed that gave him a mandate to take care of the place. He once refused to allow a carnival to set up in town because there had been a drought that year and field workers had not had much cotton to chop and pick. He felt they needed all the money they

CHAPTER NINE

had to feed and clothe their families. And he had been known to padlock a local business when he caught men gambling and drinking illegal beverages on its premises. He ran a clean county.

In *Echoes from the Rio Grande* (p. 209), John R. Peavey commented on conditions in Hebbronville in 1923: "Hebbronville . . . was a quiet little western cow town with its friendly easy going people, the 'Last Chance Barber Shop' and the old wooden railroad station and the cattle shipping pens. There wasn't a saloon or gambling house in town, a striking contrast by comparison to San Diego."

Pell hired a man named Modesto Guerra to work their newly acquired land. He had been farming on T. T. East's San Antonio Viejo Ranch, but Mr. East had decided to stop farming.

Modesto knew a little about carpentry, and as the Harbison land had no buildings on it, he built a house for himself and his wife, Andalia, and their ten children on one of the low hills.

Pell also bought from the East ranch four mules and some farming equipment. He told Modesto not to work a span of mules more than half a day at a time. He didn't want his mules abused.

Helen wanted to plant lots of cotton and corn. Pell thought land was meant for grazing. He wanted to plant a small amount of cotton—as a money crop for Modesto—and just enough corn to feed the animals. He told Helen, "I hate to see my land plowed up."

He bought a small herd of Jersey cows and allowed Modesto's family to milk them and use the milk. And he gave Modesto's wife two turkey hens and a gobbler, and told her she could keep all the turkeys she raised except two or three that he wanted for his family at Thanksgiving and Christmas.

On November 30, 1923, Helen bore their first child. They named her Hazel Maurine. Pell was excited, and very proud. He didn't go to work at all that day. He dressed in a white shirt and his good serge suit and stayed at home all day to receive congratulations. The next day he went to Laredo and bought his new daughter a gold locket and chain. The locket had a place inside for photographs, and Pell inserted one of himself and one of Helen.

By the time Hazel was old enough to hold her head up, Pell was taking her all over town, to show her off. She soon became the darling of Hebbronville. When the Rangers were in town, they were always either bringing her gifts or taking her to the drugstore for treats. One of them gave her a doll that had three heads that could be screwed on

With Pell

and off, with different costumes for each head. There was a long white dress for the baby head, a gingham dress and bonnet for the head that had red hair, and a dress of pink lace for the blonde head. Even the Catholic priest took Hazel to the store and told her he'd buy her anything she saw there that she liked. What she chose that time was a toy brush, comb, and mirror set. If Helen and Pell had not already been a favorite couple in the little town, Hazel would have made them so.

When she was seven months old, Helen caught her with her hand in the fish bowl, trying to catch a goldfish, and Helen got a snapshot of that. It won for her first place in a national contest sponsored by Kodak and Fox Studios. The prize was $100.

Modesto's daughter Eva worked for Helen after Hazel was born, helping to care for the house and the baby. That allowed Helen time to work in her flower garden, and to participate in such local social affairs as lawn parties at the Henry Edds home — the only home in Hebbronville that had grass in its yard — teas and luncheons in the dining room of the Hotel Viggo, and meetings of the Self Culture Club, where ladies got together to crochet, embroider, and talk.

As Hazel became older, Helen read to her and told stories and drew pictures for her.

Protestant Sunday school and church services were held in the courthouse. One Sunday, the Baptists. The next Sunday, the Methodists. The next Sunday, maybe some other denomination. Sunday school was held every Sunday, preaching less regularly. All denominations attended each Sunday, no matter which denomination was in charge. Pell went with Helen a couple of times when they were first married; then he balked. When Hazel was old enough, Helen took her every Sunday and just left Pell at home.

Two and one-half years after Hazel was born, the Harbisons' second child arrived. They named her Georgia Isabel. With two little girls, Pell was doubly pleased. Ever since losing his mother and brother and sister in the tornado in Goliad, he had yearned for a family. His need seemed to be great. Now, it was being appeased.

One night when Helen was up with one of the children, she heard noises in the street at the front of the house. There was a truck out there, apparently stuck in the sand. Pell went to the door and called, "¿Que paso?"

A man called back, *"Yo estoy atascado"* (I'm stuck).

CHAPTER NINE

Pell asked where he was from. The man said he was from across the border and that he was trying to get to San Diego.

Well, that gave him away, right then—all *mescaleros* headed for San Diego, the county seat of Duval County. Pell expected to find him driving an ancient, battered truck loaded with mescal or tequila. He told him he would get dressed and come out there.

To his surprise, when he approached the truck he saw it was a brand-new International. This was interesting. May be the man wasn't a *mescalero* after all. But when Pell asked what he was carrying, the fellow whispered, "Tequila."

"You just played hell! I'm the sheriff." Pell took the man and locked him in jail.

The next day Pell and some of the other law enforcement officers smashed the bottles of tequila, but not before Helen snapped a picture of Hazel beside a huge demijohn that was as big as she was. The new truck joined the stock of confiscated articles.

Although Pell had refused to attend Sunday school with Helen and Hazel, now that Helen was occupied with baby Georgia he dressed up every Sunday and took Hazel to Sunday school and sat with her until it was over. He did it until Helen could go again; then he was through with that.

One of the local women tried to shame him into going to church, saying, "It's going to be mighty lonesome up there in heaven without you."

Pell said, "Oh, I'm gonna be there. Miss Helen"—he had stopped calling her Skeeter and started calling her Miss Helen after they were married—"Miss Helen told me when we got married we became one person. Now everybody knows Miss Helen is going to heaven. And I figure if we're one person she's gonna have to take me with her wherever she goes."

One year and two days after Georgia was born, the Harbisons celebrated the birth of their son Reginald Newton, on May 21, 1927. It was another day for being proud. Alleene came to help care for the house and the children. She started calling the baby boy "Bubs," and from then on that was the only name he had, so far as the family was concerned.

In the spring of 1928 Helen and Pell built a house on their ranch, and in April he resigned his position as sheriff and they moved to the ranch—to start long years of hard work, through good times and bad.

CHAPTER TEN

Helen and Pell planned their ranch house carefully. She was responsible for the floor plan, he for the construction itself. The house was one story, with a living room, dining room, kitchen, three bedrooms, a bath, and a large gallery across the front. It was of Spanish design, with arched windows and gallery.

Pell employed C. F. Luque to build the house. In 1915 Mr. Luque had built the Hotel Viggo in Hebbronville, constructing it of poured concrete. Pell wanted his ranch house built that way. He wanted every part of it made of poured concrete—floor, walls, roof—and he wanted it reinforced with steel rods. He knew Mr. Luque knew how to do that.

The walls, partitions, roof, and floor of the house were made seven inches thick, reinforced with "sucker" rods salvaged from the junk pile at one of the oil fields. The exterior walls were set directly on the caliche that underlies the several feet of topsoil. Caliche is a loosely consolidated, rocklike formation that is found in many semi-arid places. At the Harbison ranch it is composed mostly of calcium carbonate, mixed with sand and clay, and is buried under from three to eight feet of sandy loam. It has a caprock that is as hard as concrete, so it made a perfect foundation for Pell's indestructible house. The gravel used for the house was given to Pell and Helen by W. W. Jones, from a creek on his land.

Pell's hired man, Modesto, had once worked at building wheels—for wagons, and for the big-wheeled carts that were used for many years to transport freight along the Rio Grande. He built the forms for the arches Pell wanted in the design of his house.

Helen and Pell went to Mexico and bought hand-decorated tile for the floor of the living and dining rooms.

Under the kitchen they built a storm cellar that could be entered from either the kitchen or the yard. Any time there was a bad storm, Pell brought his Mexican help to the big house. And he put his family

CHAPTER TEN

regularly through storm drills, similar to the fire drills held at schools. He wanted them to get to that cellar in case of a storm. He didn't want to lose them as he had lost his mother and his brother and sister.

Their house was a source of pride for them, and a topic of conversation among their friends. It not only was a safe place for their family, it was an excellent investment. It would cost them practically nothing in upkeep. They did not even feel that they needed insurance—no storm or fire could destroy that house.

The earliest structures in Jim Hogg County had been built of stone, and they survived. The house on the E. L. Armstrongs' El Sordo Ranch was made of huge blocks of rock that were hauled by ox cart all the way from Randado, fifteen miles south of there. The large ranch house at La Partición, where Helen taught school for three months in the summer of 1918, was built of stone. And there were a few other old stone buildings in the county.

Almost all the buildings in Hebbronville were constructed of wood. A few were made of brick. Hebbronville had come into being after the railroad was built across the area in the early 1880s, and after brick and lumber could be brought in by train. It became practical, and fashionable, to build with lumber. The large and elegant homes belonging to Oscar Thompson and Henry Edds were built of wood, as were the houses and other buildings on such important ranches as W. W. Jones's Alta Vista and Reuben Holbein's Las Cuatas. And of course the house Helen grew up in at Tipperary Farm was built of wood.

The day the Harbisons moved from town to the ranch was a wild, disorganized time. Alleene had come to help. She was a neat person, accustomed to having things orderly. When they finished breakfast, she started to pack the pots and pans and dishes. After that she planned to strip the beds and pack the linens, then to pack pictures and whatnots. She told Helen to attend to the three children and pack the clothes. Pell had told them he would send some pickup trucks to move them, that he'd be waiting for them at the ranch.

Alleene thought she had it all organized. But before she had finished packing the kitchen things, the trucks began to arrive in front of the house. Men came in and began snatching up furniture, pulling pictures from the walls, rolling up bedding, carrying out mattresses. As soon as one truck was filled, another one pulled up. Everything was scooped up and loaded, haphazardly. Finally thirteen truckloads had been sent on their way to the ranch. Helen, Alleene, and the children

With Pell

followed in a car. Alleene declared she had never seen such disorder.

On the way to the ranch, over the sandy, rutted road, Helen's new kitchen cabinet—with the porcelain enamel counter top that pulled out to make a table, the flour bin that was enclosed in the upper left side and had its own built-in sifter, the shelves for dishes, and the drawers for towels and silverware—that lovely kitchen cabinet fell from the truck and was broken to pieces. Everything else arrived in fairly good condition, and eventually they were settled in their new home.

Pell added to his herd of Jerseys and started a small dairy. He ordered a cream separator and bolted it to the floor of the kitchen so Helen could separate the cream from the milk in the comfort of the house and away from the flies, because their new house had screens at the windows and doors.

They bought a barrel churn that held enough cream to make sixteen pounds of butter. They got an ice box that held 300 pounds of ice, and they bought ice every other day from a man named Ash Creacy, who delivered it to the ranches and the oil fields.

Delivering ice was Ash's chief occupation, but ice wasn't all he delivered. He carried messages, mailed letters, and found space in his truck for everything from birthday cakes to boxes of new-born chickens. He was a link with civilization for the isolated people on his route.

Pell and Helen got up at three o'clock every morning. While he and Modesto did the milking, Helen cooked breakfast.

After Pell went to the field, Helen separated the milk, cooled the cream, did the day's churning, and processed the butter. She had learned butter making from her mother, who had learned it from her own mother. It was hard work. She washed away all the buttermilk with ice water; then she had to work the water out with a wooden paddle. And she had to know how much salt to work into the butter. She molded it in a one-pound wooden mold, wrapped it in a strong, thin paper especially made for that purpose, and packed it in her personally designed butter cartons that said "Hebbronville Butter, made by Mrs. P. B. Harbison." She had a ready market in Hebbronville and the oil fields for all the butter she could make. The year was 1929. Ed Lasater was already operating his famous dairy at Falfurrias, in the adjoining county.

When the Harbison ranch house was built, it was wired for electric lights, one outlet in the ceiling of each room, no outlets for appliances of any kind. At first they used kerosene lamps, but soon Pell

CHAPTER TEN

bought a 32-volt Delco Remy light plant that was powered by a gasoline engine. It had sixteen large 2-volt glass batteries and was located in the back yard in a small building they called the power house. It furnished electricity for lights at the house and the barn, and for operating a radio.

That spring Helen persuaded Pell to plow up additional land for corn and cotton. Modesto began planting cotton on February 16. It was a good year. The rains came at the right time and there was no trouble with frost. They got a beautiful cotton crop. Helen could hardly stay out of the field. She had been watching one particular spot where the cotton stalks were big. Two stalks had nearly 100 bolls each. She tied strips of cloth to those two and told Pell not to allow anybody to pick them. She wanted to enter them in a contest that Sears, Roebuck was sponsoring as part of an advertising campaign to sell seed. The prize for the best stalk of cotton was $3,000.

When the cotton was ready, Pell hired pickers from Salineño, a little community to the south, and turned them loose in the field. By Friday noon they had enough cotton to make a bale. Helen urged Pell to take it to Hebbronville immediately, as there was a prize for the first bale of cotton to be ginned. But he didn't do it. He said he would wait until the next day.

Late Friday afternoon a farmer who lived near them took a load of cotton to the gin!

And, to make matters worse, when Helen went to get her two prize stalks of cotton she found them bare; all the bolls had been picked. She felt very frustrated. She wanted to stomp, and kick, and yell, and blame Pell. But she knew he would pout for days if she hurt his feelings. She was learning to try to be careful about that.

By the late 1920s many Mexicans had crossed the border, one way or another. Ranchers found workers plentiful. The Harbisons always had at least one Mexican family living on the ranch. The men helped with the heavy farming, and the other members of the family who were old enough helped with the milking, chopped and picked cotton, did chores. Helen almost always had one or two of the girls working in the house and looking after the Harbison children. They were better as babysitters than as maids. If Helen was away from the house, they'd play the Victrola and dance instead of sweeping and washing dishes.

Just as Pell had run a clean town and county when he was sheriff,

With Pell

he and Helen were strict with the way they ran their ranch. Pell was just as authoritarian as ever; his brown eyes could still look a hole through a person. He never hit one of his employees, but he tolerated no back talk. And another thing he didn't tolerate was wife beating. His son Reginald said of him, "He'd run a man off as quick as look at him." As for liquor, they kept the ranch dry. Pell was not averse to drinking in moderation. Helen was against it in any form. Neither of them wanted any whiskey on the ranch. They didn't bring it there, and they didn't allow anybody else to.

Pell did not want Helen to work in the field, so she planted and cared for a two-acre vegetable and flower garden. Pell prepared the soil for her, but she planted it and kept the weeds down by working with a hoe. She said to herself, "Here I go, following in Mama's footsteps."

Helen was pregnant again, expecting the baby sometime the last part of January, 1930. Pell was in high spirits, as he always was when they were expecting another baby. Neither he nor Helen were concerned that operating the separator and the heavy churn might be too much for a pregnant woman. Helen knew that turning the separator made her uncomfortable but she thought discomfort was all it would cause — she thought she could do whatever she put her mind to.

It was unusually warm during the Christmas holidays in 1929, and on December 28 it turned really hot. Helen separated the milk and churned. She had trouble getting the milk worked out of the butter that day because the temperature was so high that the butter stayed soft.

Their little 32-volt generator was always giving them trouble. It was not working the evening of December 28, and Pell had gotten Charley Roddy out there to repair it. After they got the generator going, Pell and Charley sat in the living room and talked for a long time, just visiting. Pell knew Helen had gone to bed, and he assumed she was all right.

Helen was not all right. She had started having labor pains. She should not have been having them — the baby was not due for another month. The pains got harder and closer together, and Helen knew she needed to tell Pell about it, but she was too shy to go and tell him, in front of that other man.

Finally the man was gone, and Pell went to Hebbronville for Dr. Stetson. The doctor he came back with was new in the county. Dr. Stetson was not in town that night.

In the meantime a norther had blown in and the temperature was

CHAPTER TEN

dropping fast. By the time the baby was born, the house was cold. Houses in Jim Hogg County didn't need heat much of the time. The Harbisons' house had no heat in the bedrooms. It was heated by a fireplace in the living room and a wood cookstove in the kitchen. Conditions were not good for the survival of a premature baby.

The baby was a girl. They named her Donia Ione. She lived only a few hours.

Helen almost died also. She hemorrhaged until she was near death. Then she developed blood poisoning. She was anemic and weak for months afterward. They hired a young woman named Covie Medford as a housekeeper, and Covie later married Helen's brother Howard.

Helen and Pell believed that the heavy work Helen had been doing caused the baby to be born prematurely. Pell moved the separator to the barn and started selling cream to J. C. Walker of the Laredo Creamery. The only butter Helen made now was for her own family.

Ike and Mattie had gone back to Tipperary Farm for a few years after Helen and Pell were married, but in 1930 they leased the farm and moved into Helen's house in Hebbronville. Mattie still had a big garden, no matter where she lived.

Helen was depressed for many months after the birth, and death, of little Donia Ione. Pell tried desperately to help her regain her former zest. One time he ran a bunch of calves through the back door and all the way through the house and out the front door, hoping she would find that amusing. She did laugh, just to please him.

Pell started a small herd of range cattle. He liked to work with that kind of cattle. He didn't like dairying, but he tolerated the dairy because it was a continuous source of income, whereas beef cattle and farming brought in money only once a year.

There were numerous dairy herds in Jim Hogg County in the 1930s, and most dairymen used silos for preserving and storing cane and other forage crops that they fed their cows. These were not the tall, cylindrical structures seen on farms in the northern states; they were pits or trenches that were dug into the ground. This was practical for several reasons: the cost of building them was less, it was relatively easy to protect their contents from contact with the air, and they could not be blown down by hurricanes or tornados.

Pell hired some men to dig a silo beside the dairy barn. They used mules and a scoop to remove the several feet of sandy loam and clay that lay above the caliche caprock. The caprock was so hard it had to be blasted with dynamite, but once they had removed that they could use picks and shovels to loosen the underlying caliche so they could remove it with the scoop. Pieces of the caprock, held together by adobe mortar, were used to shore up the unconsolidated soil above the caliche and thus form the uppermost part of the trench, or silo.

Even before Reginald was big enough to work in the field, he was usually right at his father's heels, watching everything that went on. Of silos and ensilage, he says:

> Our main ensilage crop was cane. We raised some corn. But corn did not make as much tonnage as cane.
>
> At first we had the cane harvested by men using machetes. I remember Marcos Mejillos and his two sons cut cane for us.
>
> Later, we contracted the cane cutting to a man who used a row binder that was pulled by mules. The iron wheels of the binder powered the cutting mechanism — a knife that cut the cane off near the ground. The binder held the cane until it accumulated enough for a bundle, which it automatically tied with binding twine and dropped off.
>
> The bundles were picked up and hauled in a wagon to the silo, where the cane was run through an ensilage cutter that chopped it up and blew it into the silo. Once in the silo, the chopped cane was sprinkled with water, compacted, and covered with about eight inches of dirt. It then went through a pickling process which cured it and turned it into ensilage. That took about two or three weeks. Once cured in this way, ensilage will keep for several years. We used it when no fresh feed was available, usually in the winter or during a drought.
>
> When we were ready to feed the ensilage to the cows, we dug it out of the trench silo by hand, with a twelve-tined pitchfork, and carried it in galvanized tubs or a small trailer to the feeding troughs. But before we dug it we had to shovel the layer of dirt off the top. A thin layer of cane was also dug off and discarded, because at the contact with the dirt, and also at the contact with the walls of the silo, there was usually some mold on the ensilage.
>
> The ensilage cutter was powered by an old Fordson tractor that we used only for its power take-off. The pulley on the power take-off drove a six- or eight-inch belt that drove the cutter and conveyor on the ensilage cutter.
>
> When we were harvesting the cane and filling the silos in the late 1930s and early 1940s, we employed anywhere from eight to twenty-

CHAPTER TEN

five men — depending on whether we had the cane cut by hand or by the mule-drawn row binder. Now, in 1985, one man with one tractor, towing an ensilage cutter and self-unloading trailer, can do the job. But the one-man job is not cost effective today. People are feeding hay that is put up in those large round bales and is distributed in the pastures. But the hay is not as good as ensilage for feeding cattle. Cows love that sweet-smelling mash that comes out of a silo. And for milk production, it is as valuable as new grass.

Before they were old enough to go to school, the Harbison children lived in isolation with their parents and the Mexican help. They were usually with Pell when he was working near the house or in the barnyard, fixing fence, building gates, working on the farm machinery. They ran his errands, handed him his tools. He called them his little shirttails.

They grew up speaking the form of Spanish called Tex-Mex. They often sneaked off and went to play with the Mexican children. This was against their mother's orders, and they got switched for it when she caught them. But they never stopped doing it. Georgia said, "The fun was worth the switching."

Helen did not object to her children's playing with the little Mexicans. She was merely concerned for their safety and didn't want them running wild all over the ranch. The Mexican children came to the ranch house to play with her children, with her blessing. And they often helped themselves to food in her kitchen when her back was turned. Sometimes when one of them was eating a sweet potato or a cupcake, a brother or sister would hold a tea towel in front of the little one's face, believing that would conceal from Helen the fact that the child was eating something.

Sometimes the Harbison children and their Mexican friends played hide and seek in the evenings, rattlesnakes and all. About the only thing that frightened them was a coyote. That was because they had been told tales about rabid coyotes. Sometimes Pell would run with them at night, in the pasture in front of the ranch house, and when he had led them out a little way he would yell "Coyote!" and act as if he was going to run to the house and leave them.

After a rain the children played in the puddles and pretended they were swimming. When Helen complained of their muddy clothes and bodies, they told her they loved to smell the earth after a rain. She didn't chastise them further — she knew that feeling.

With Pell

Pell taught them to save string and hang it on the fence for the birds to use in building their nests. And he sometimes brought them a baby rabbit he found in the field.

Helen read to them and told them stories. She drew and painted with them. She often took them outside to look at the stars at night. She told them about the time she had watched Halley's comet, and about the time she and her father drove through the myriad of fireflies.

No school bus came down Randado Road in those days, so when the Harbison children were old enough to go to school they had to live with Helen's parents in Hebbronville during the week and come home only on weekends. Georgia, particularly, didn't like to do that—she loved to be at home.

Modesto moved his family to town, to put his children in school, and Pell hired a single man to take his place. The man wanted to get married but he had a problem. It was the custom for a Mexican man to buy the trousseau for his bride, but this young man didn't have any money. Pell ran an account at the Francisco Gutierrez store in Hebbronville, so he told the man to allow his bride to go there and get her trousseau. She bought the best of everything, and ran up a bill of over one hundred dollars. When Pell showed his surprise, the man said, "She is not mine yet, and I can't say what she can have. It will be different after we are married." And it *was* different. That fine trousseau was all the pretty clothes the wife ever got. She never had any other luxuries. All she had was hard work. She bore a child every year, working in the field right up to the time her babies were born.

Pell and Helen never got another cotton crop to equal the one they raised in 1929. The infestation of the boll weevil grew steadily worse. Helen begged Pell to poison the cotton but he would not. He wouldn't allow any kind of poison on the ranch. He didn't want to raise cotton, anyhow. He hated cotton. Helen couldn't understand that. She loved cotton. She loved to pick the fluffy white bolls, and she did pick a bit sometimes, in spite of Pell's wanting her not to work in the field.

Months after she lost her baby, Helen was still plagued by depression. She started writing poetry and composing songs to try to take her mind off her hurt. In one of the newspapers she saw an advertisement by something called the Indiana Song Bureau, asking people to submit song lyrics for possible publication, and she sent off a song she called "Longing for a Light to Turn My Way." They wrote her and said the lyrics had excellent possibilities, that they had set them to mu-

CHAPTER TEN

sic and had gotten a "student" to sing the song and record it. They sent Helen a recording of her song and told her it had been broadcast over radio station WRGN. They said they were getting it copyrighted. They warned her not to get in touch with anybody else about the song, naming several groups or companies—including one called the National Song Bureau (New York)—they said she should not have anything to do with.

Helen was ecstatic. She was sure the Indiana Song Bureau was reputable and that she was going to be famous. But when she received a contract to sign, Pell was apprehensive. He refused to allow her to sign it.

She never completely forgave him.

CHAPTER ELEVEN

It seemed that every time Helen was at her mother's house in town she wanted to look something up in Mattie's big doctor book. Finally Mattie told her, "Just take it, you need it worse than I do."

Helen was pleased to get the book. For one thing she felt nostalgic about it. It had been an important item in the home all the time she was growing up. Also, it would be very helpful. It was comprehensive. It discussed all the common—and some of the not-so-common—ailments and offered suggestions for treating them. She depended upon it from then on, not only in caring for her own family but also in doctoring children of workers on the ranch. There were even times when she believed it was a lifesaver.

Once a two-year-old child drank kerosene that had been left in a Coca-Cola bottle on the floor. When the parents brought the baby to the ranch house, it was pale and limp, and reeking of kerosene. Helen, remembering that she had seen emetics discussed in the doctor book, quickly found the page and read the instructions. She forced the baby to drink dry mustard mixed with warm water and then ran her finger down its throat. The kerosene came up, and the patient recovered.

Another child she believed she saved was a baby with an infected navel cord. It was born to an itinerant family that was working on the ranch. By the time they brought it to Helen its temperature was 105 degrees.

It had been delivered by a midwife who evidently had given it little attention. She had not bathed it, and she had left several inches of the navel cord attached. Its problems were multiplied by the naïveté and superstitions of its parents. The weather was hot, but the child was dressed in several layers of clothes, even had three caps on its head.

Helen took charge. She stripped it and gave it an enema. Then she bathed it, cut off the infected end of the long cord, and sprinkled the

CHAPTER ELEVEN

navel with boric acid powder. She wrapped the baby in a band she had used for her own infants, and took a bottle and nipple from the cabinet and gave it some water. "The parents thought they weren't supposed to give it any water."

Helen had the pleasure of seeing that baby, a few years later, grown into a healthy child.

Another time, a little Mexican boy burned his feet in hot coals, just as Helen had done that time at Tipperary Farm. She didn't need to read the doctor book in order to know what to do this time. Remembering well the remedy her mother had gotten from the book, all those years ago, she applied a poultice of grated raw Irish potatoes.

In the spring of 1931 Helen was pregnant again. Pell was delighted. Not only could they look forward to another little Harbison, but Helen's melancholy was slipping away as she nurtured the new life within her.

They continued to plant cotton, and the boll weevils continued to destroy a good portion of it because Pell would not poison it. But they always had at least some cotton to sell. Sometimes Pell would allow the children to climb on top of the truckload of soft cotton and ride to the gin. When he did, he took along one of the ranch hands to babysit.

During the last week in July Pell took the children to Mattie, and Helen to Laredo to await the birth of the baby they expected around the first of August. This time the birth would be in a hospital. They didn't want a repeat of the trouble they had a year and a half ago, when they lost little Donia Ione. Helen boarded with a friend of the family who had a house near the hospital.

On August 5, 1931, Alice Louise was born in Mercy Hospital. There were no problems. They had another beautiful, healthy little girl. That made four fine children. Hazel was seven, Georgia was five, Reginald four.

And by the spring of 1934 they were blissfully looking forward to another addition to the herd of little Harbisons. As she was wont to do, Helen expressed her feelings in poetry:

Spring's Secret

Spring is beginning to quicken the presence of
    the flower and the bee,
Spring is beginning to whisper a little secret
    to me,

With Pell

> A secret that I've been guessing and blessing,
>   too:
> Spring is beginning to tell me I'll soon have a
>   dream come true.
> Little garments I'm sewing so dainty and downy
>   and white—
> Love in my heart is growing with such a dream
>   so bright—
> Dreaming and wondering and guessing, if eyes will be
>   brown or blue,
> If a lad or a lassie the blessing, and will it be
>   one or two?

Helen's dream came true, and her questions were all answered on April 18, 1934. Ida Alleene was born at the hospital in Laredo. The birth was easy; the child was healthy and beautiful. Helen and Pell were happy and proud.

But no matter how well things were going on the ranch, there was almost always something to cope with, and that spring Helen encountered an unusually annoying problem—ground squirrels invaded her garden. They took a few bites of this, a few of that, ruining everything. She was frustrated, and furious. She had worked too hard to have it all destroyed. Besides, she needed the vegetables to feed her family. Pell had forbidden her to use any kind of poison on the ranch. But she was desperate. When she was in Hebbronville she bought grain that had been treated with nux vomica, a strychnine-like poison that kills its victims in a few minutes. As soon as she felt she could do it without Pell's catching her she used it.

The ground squirrels dug tunnels into the loose soil, leaving mounds of sand here and there where they entered the ground, so Helen had no trouble finding places to deposit her poisoned grain where a man walking casually in the garden would not notice it. She hurried. Pell had gone to town that morning, but he had not planned to stay long. She took time to pull a weed or two here and there—she couldn't bear to go on and leave those weeds once she'd seen them—and by the time she was on the last row she had spent more time than she expected to.

At the end of the garden was a place where the dog had dug into a ground squirrel nest. Helen still had a big handful of the poisoned grain that she wanted to get rid of. She pushed her hand into the hole in order to drop the grain where it couldn't be seen, and came in con-

CHAPTER ELEVEN

tact with something soft. She stood back to let the sunlight into the hole. Now she could see what she had just had her hand on. It was a big coiled rattlesnake. It apparently was asleep, probably full of ground squirrel.

Helen forgot everything except the snake. She went to the house and got the shotgun and shot it.

As she was pulling it out of the hole, Pell walked up. He looked at the bits of grain all over the snake and around on the ground and said, "I didn't know they were filling shotgun shells with poison wheat these days."

If Helen and Pell had been going to part company over things like this, they would have done it long before that day.

By now, ten-year-old Hazel was reading to the younger children and telling them stories, following a pattern her mother had established, building a tradition.

Pell was protective of his daughters. He wouldn't allow them to ride horses, for fear they might get hurt. They didn't go to the barn, and they didn't work in the fields. But he started treating his only son like a man when he was hardly more than a baby.

Reginald was allowed to hang around the dairy barn and the Mexican men who worked there almost as soon as he was able to toddle over there. By the time he was six he was going to the barn every time his father did, and he was learning to milk. At first he milked only a tin cupful and drank it. But soon he was milking his own cow. Pell and the hired hands bragged on him. He learned to milk. And he learned to cuss. Pell never chastised him for cussing, but he had to be careful about it around the house—if one of the girls heard him she was likely to run to Helen with, "Mama, Bubs said a bad word."

Once, when he was "helping" his father build a gate, Pell said, "Bubs, you know that little saw I keep in that cabinet at the house?"

"Yes."

"Well, run up there and get me that son-of-a-bitch."

When Reginald found he couldn't get the saw out of the cabinet, he yelled back to his father, "Daddy. . . . I can't reach the son-of-a-bitch."

Helen came to get the saw for him, and to lecture him about his language: "No wonder you couldn't get the saw down. Cussing like that! You must learn to speak properly; that's the way to be effective."

Reginald said, "Daddy cusses. And he builds good gates."

Reginald had his own horse and saddle from the time he was eight

With Pell

or nine, and he herded cattle right along with the men. Pell put what are called "tapaderos" on his son's stirrups. That is a strip of leather across the front of the stirrup to keep a rider's foot from slipping through and getting caught. Reginald recalled, "I was thrown a few times, and certain parts of my anatomy suffered, but I never got dragged."

As much as she could, Helen filled her life with things she enjoyed —her family, her garden, writing poetry, even picking cotton when she could sneak off to the field without Pell's knowing it.

She had to cook three meals a day, and although she didn't exactly love to cook, she didn't mind it. She served nourishing meals to her family, and often to field hands as well. Their diet consisted of lots of vegetables from her garden, chicken, and pork sausage that they made every two or three months and fried and packed in lard. They cured their own hams and bacon. She made biscuits for every meal. They had fruit from their own peach, plum, grapefruit, orange, and lemon trees. They seldom had beef. Even a small calf produced more meat than they could eat before some of it spoiled—their only cooling appliance was a kerosene refrigerator.

The few things she didn't enjoy doing, she tried to avoid as much as possible. She'd say, "I just wasn't cut out for that."

And one of the things she wasn't cut out for was keeping a tidy house. It seemed so futile. It never stayed straight as long as it took her to straighten it.

Once when things were in more disarray than usual—with doll clothes and childrens' clothes, story books, crayons, and toys strewn over the floor and the chairs—Pell looked out the front door and said, "I think I see Mrs. Oscar Thompson's car at the gate."

Well. That set things moving. Ever since 1912, when she lived with the Thompsons and went to school in Hebbronville, Helen had loved Mrs. Thompson and felt close to her, but she had always been in awe of her. The house was never so straight as when she knew Mrs. Thompson was coming to visit. Pell's announcement electrified her now. She started stuffing things into closets and behind bedroom doors. In a very few minutes the place was surprisingly neat. Pell looked out the door again and said he guessed he had been mistaken—must have been the sun shining on the mail box—wasn't any car in sight. Then he sat in his uncluttered chair in the nice straight living room, picked up the newspaper and began nonchalantly to read.

At one time the Harbisons had some little Mexican girls living on

CHAPTER ELEVEN

the ranch who were forever stealing eggs from the hen house and carrying them home in the baggy legs of their bloomers. The awkward way the girls waddled along when their bloomer legs were full of eggs made it easy to know when they had been visiting the hens' nests. Reginald once ran behind them, whacking them around the legs with a stick until a stream of broken eggs cascaded down their legs and left a trail behind them on the ground.

Pell's only relatives besides Helen and the children were two older brothers who had survived the tornado in Goliad along with Pell. Clyde was sheriff and tax collector of Goliad County for seventeen years, and Earle was treasurer of Victoria County for a long time. Clyde and his wife, Carrie, had one child, a son named Malcolm. Earle and his wife, Mettie, who had no children, came to visit once and brought Helen's children a little chair that was a family heirloom. Helen considered the chair a prize possession because it came from Pell's family. She took a photograph of two-year-old Alice sitting in it, holding her doll, and the picture turned out so well she decided to enter it in a contest at the 1933 World's Fair in Chicago. It won her a gold medal. That wasn't quite as exciting as when she won $100 for the photograph of Hazel with her hand in the fish bowl, but it was another important accomplishment just the same.

One year, Georgia set some eggs under a guinea hen and hatched several baby guineas that she was very fond of. Her devotion to the little guineas amused her parents, until one time she awakened them in the middle of the night, saying something was bothering her guineas. They told her to go back to bed, that she had been dreaming. But Georgia refused to leave their room. She began to cry. Helen, annoyed and exasperated, finally got out of bed and took a flashlight and went with Georgia to the hen house, to prove to her that the guineas were all right.

To Helen's amazement, there in the guinea coop was a big chicken snake, swallowing the baby guineas. Helen killed the snake. It was not poisonous — it was dangerous only to Georgia's guineas and other things it could swallow. They pulled one little guinea from the snake's mouth. It had a broken leg, but it survived.

But shortly after that they had an encounter with a snake that was life-threatening to more than guineas. Hazel and Georgia were playing under a grapefruit tree beside the house. Helen had not heard them for a while and went to see what they were doing. To her horror, there they sat, staring at a large, coiled rattlesnake that was staring back at

With Pell

them. Helen tried to kill the snake with a hoe, but the hoe kept bouncing off of it. She finally had to call for help from a Mexican woman who was doing the laundry, and together they managed to kill it. Hazel said later that she had been sitting there for some time, staring at the snake, getting sleepy.

After the death of J. P. Reed, the Trap—where Mr. Reed nurtured and rested his cattle before he shipped them, and where Pell and Alec Reed had taken Helen and Garland on that first date—was for sale. There were 307 acres of it. Pell bought it. He may have wanted it for nostalgic reasons. Not only had it figured in his first date with Helen, it had been important to Mr. Reed, who had been like a father to Pell after he was orphaned by the storm in Goliad.

Hazel seemed to have inherited her mother's talent for story telling. By the time she was ten or eleven she was entertaining the younger Harbisons with stories she made up as she went along. Pell and Helen always took a nap after lunch, and it was then that Hazel usually told her stories—to keep the little ones quiet.

Also, as Hazel and Georgia got older, they took over much of the work around the house, such as dishwashing, laundry, cleaning, babysitting. Sometimes it got a little much. When they felt the need to get away from it all, Hazel would tell Georgia, "Meet me in the park."

The "park" was a playhouse Hazel had built around the runoff from the kitchen sink—the closest thing she could find to a flowing stream. She made little benches and planted flowers. She even built a small bridge across the runoff. When the day had been particularly hectic, Hazel would slip a couple of stemmed glasses from the cabinet and a bottle of Coca-Cola from the kerosene refrigerator—she had to be sly about it because the Harbison children were not permitted to have drinks that contained caffeine—and the two girls would retire to the park and sit on a bench and smell the flowers and gaze at the trickle of water under the little bridge and pretend it was a river, the Coca-Cola was wine, and they were elegant ladies.

The last of August, 1936, Helen went to Laredo to await the birth of what turned out to be their last child. Pell kept Hazel and the two youngest girls at the ranch with him, but he took Reginald and Georgia to Mattie. Hazel was only twelve, but she was expected to care for two-year-old Ida and five-year-old Alice and to do all the cooking and housekeeping. Hazel said, "It would have been considered improper in that community at that time to have a maid live there in the house

CHAPTER ELEVEN

when Mother was gone, even with us children there. And no Mexican woman would have done it."

On September 9, 1936, Carrie Lee was born. She grew into a delightful child that people said looked and acted just like Helen.

The years were passing. Helen and Pell had worked hard. They had never had a lot of money, but they had always been able to afford what they needed. They had paid cash for the Harbison ranch when they bought it, and they had never used it as security for borrowed money. They told themselves they never would, they'd always keep it safe. They owned the Trap now. If they ever needed to put up land as security they'd put up the Trap.

During the Depression of the 1930s dairy prices fell—a five-gallon can of heavy cream brought only five dollars—but prices for what they had to buy went down also. And the Harbisons didn't need to buy very much. They raised most of the food for the people and animals on their ranch. Dairy farmers in Jim Hogg County felt the effects of the Depression less than did most people in the United States. For Helen and Pell, life didn't change much. Although the three older children were growing up, they still had three little girls who were not much more than babies to come and kiss them goodnight. And Pell still had little shirttails to do his errands and run herd on his tools.

Helen took the children to Sunday school and church at the Methodist church in Hebbronville. Once in a long while Pell would condescend to accompany them. "When he did, we filled up a whole pew."

Three times a day, except on school days, Pell and Helen and every child sat at the table for a meal—no excuses such as "I'm not hungry" or "I'll eat later." When Helen put food on the table, everybody sat there. And if it happened to be news time, the radio was switched on and everybody listened quietly to the news, whether he or she wanted to or not.

Shortly after Carrie Lee was born, Pell stopped going to the barn to help with the milking. Reginald was ten years old. For a year or more he had been milking as many cows as any of the men. He knew as much as Pell did about operating the equipment, and washing it and cleaning it up after they were through. Pell turned the dairy over to him. He and one or two hired men milked thirty cows, by hand.

From then on, Reginald went to the barn at four o'clock—every morning and every afternoon—365 days a year. According to Reginald: "Milking was only part of the chore. The cream had to be separated,

With Pell

the skim milk had to be fed to the calves and the hogs, the buckets and separator had to be washed, and the concrete floor in the barn had to be scrubbed."

Pell himself had worked hard when he was a boy. His father died when he was seven years old, and from then on he and his brothers Clyde and Earle did whatever they could to help support their mother and younger brother and sister. Pell delivered the *Saturday Evening Post,* and he went around door to door in the neighborhoods in Goliad, taking grocery orders from housewives, filling the orders, and delivering them. After the storm left him an orphan, he lived with the J. P. Reed family. But Pell was independent. He had developed the skills needed for survival. Perhaps he felt his son needed to do the same. For whatever reason, he shifted work and responsibility onto Reginald's shoulders early.

From the first year they lived on the ranch, Helen had kept books: detailed accounts of income and expenditures, names of employees, what crops were planted and when, when cattle were bought, or born, and when they were sold. She was good at it. She didn't mind doing it.

Ranchers and farmers in that area were beginning to use tractors instead of mules. Pell decided to try that. The dealer delivered the Farmall-12 to the ranch when the Harbisons were not at home, unloaded it, and just left it sitting there. Pell had never driven a tractor, and he hesitated to try to start it. Helen was impatient with his reluctance. She climbed on the tractor, started it, and took it to the field. Pell, carrying Carrie Lee in his arms, followed—walking. When he caught up with her, he put the child down and just stood and looked at her. She climbed meekly off the tractor and took her daughter and went to the house. "I shouldn't have done it. But it was a challenge. I've always loved a challenge."

In her senior year in high school Hazel, who had always been a model child and an excellent student, decided to play hookey with one of her friends. It was an unplanned, spur-of-the-moment thing. After they left school, they didn't know what to do. There was no place to go. They went to the drugstore and drank chocolate sodas, as slowly as they could, all afternoon. When they went back to school to get their books, Mr. Jones, the principal, called them into his office and said they were expelled, that they would have to bring their parents in for a conference with him before they could attend school again. Hazel:

CHAPTER ELEVEN

I was worried to death. I didn't know what I was going to do. I couldn't make myself tell Mother and Daddy that evening. Mother was driving us to school the next morning, and we were late, as we often were, and I knew she felt pressured. But I had to tell her, somehow, before we got to school. Finally, I said, "Mother, Mr. Jones wants to see you when we get to school."

She said, "What about?"

And I just couldn't tell her. I said, "I don't know."

She assumed it was because we'd been late several times. She and I walked into the office, and before Mr. Jones said a word she started yelling at him about how hard it was to get us all to school at all, with all she had to do in the mornings, and she named off the things she had to do every morning. She had to get up at three o'clock. Did he know what it was like to get up at three o'clock every morning and get breakfast for eight people—and sometimes for field hands as well—and get five children ready for school, and then drive them all the way in there? She was doing the best she could, and she was tired of hearing complaints about it. And she went on and on.

Mr. Jones kept looking at me, and I kept looking at him. When he could get a word in, he said, "I'm sorry you are upset, Mrs. Harbison. I'm sure everything will be all right." And Mother and I left his office, and she went home and I went to class. That was the last I heard about it. I guess he was so glad to be rid of Mother that he was willing to forget about me. I didn't tell Mother the truth behind that story until after I was married.

In the spring of 1940 Hazel graduated from Hebbronville High School at age sixteen, with no more problems resulting from her hookey-playing escapade. Jim Hogg County had only eleven grades of public school then, and Hazel had skipped one of those. That fall she entered Texas College of Arts and Industries at Kingsville, Texas. Helen was pleased. She had always expected her children to go to college. She had never said "*If* you go to college." It was always "*When* you go to college."

In 1941 schools all over Texas changed from eleven grades to twelve grades of secondary school. In some districts each child was expected to complete twelve grades from then on. In Jim Hogg County the students were simply moved up one grade. Only the ones starting school in 1941 and after had to complete twelve grades. All of the Harbison children except Carrie Lee were already in school, so they had only eleven grades of public school.

With Pell

By the time Reginald was fifteen years old he had been practically living at the dairy barn for nearly five years, and he was getting tired of it. He went to the barn at four o'clock in the morning and barely got through in time to get ready for school, and he went back to the barn as soon as he came home from school and worked until eight or nine o'clock that night. He didn't complain, but Helen sensed how he felt, and she sympathized with him. He had no social life at all. He couldn't attend the young people's functions at church; he couldn't participate in any extracurricular activities at school. Helen decided she had to get him out of that barn, somehow. She started to plan.

She waited until she caught Pell in the right mood, and then she said, "Wouldn't it be nice if we could move to Austin and rent a house? Georgia and Bubs could go to a better high school, where they'd have a greater selection of courses, and Hazel could go to the University of Texas and live at home. We would all be together again." Then she added, "But of course we can't. We can't just go off and leave the ranch."

She went to the kitchen and fixed supper, leaving him to his thoughts.

The next day Pell came home from town and told her, "I saw Robert Hinnant in town. He wants to lease our ranch for his son-in-law, Jack Fulbright."

Helen and Pell went to Austin and rented a house near the University of Texas campus, at 300 West 38th Street, and on August 5, 1942, they moved.

CHAPTER TWELVE

Reginald sold his horse and saddle before they left the ranch, and spent part of the money on a bicycle that he rode all over Austin, just for the fun of it. He started to Sunday school at the Methodist church and was soon involved in an active social life.

The children were all enrolled in school. Hazel, who was almost nineteen, went to the University of Texas, living at home. Georgia, sixteen, and Reginald, fifteen, were in high school. Eleven-year-old Alice was in seventh grade; Ida, eight, was in fourth; and Carrie Lee, six, was of course in the first grade.

Helen was kept busy with the cleaning, laundry, and cooking.

Everybody was happy except Pell. He sat around the house all day and waited for Helen to get through with her work so she could go for a walk with him. Helen was surprised that he did not adjust to living in Austin. But apparently he could not. He missed people who knew him. He had left all of his prestige back in Jim Hogg County. Nobody called him "Mr. Pell." He wasn't accomplishing anything, wasn't producing anything. He felt insecure driving a car in the city, so Helen did the driving.

Pell and Helen were not accustomed to spending money for rent. The more they thought about it the more it bothered them—it was money gone, money they had no hope of getting back. They started looking for a house to buy, and when they found one they liked they went to Hebbronville and sold Helen's house to Ike and Mattie and brought the money back to Austin, prepared to buy their house.

They were disappointed. The house had been sold the day before. They continued to rent.

One Sunday afternoon they drove out to the airport to watch the planes comes and go. Pell was wearing his khakis, his custom-made boots, and his Stetson. Helen recalled, "He made a striking figure."

With Pell

A man came up and introduced himself, saying he was a judge on the Texas Supreme Court. When he learned that Pell had been a Texas Ranger and a sheriff as well as a rancher, he said a vacancy had just turned up on the state board of pardons, and he wondered whether Pell might like to be considered for it. Pell said he might. The judge suggested that Pell drop by his office and talk about it sometime soon.

The next day Helen persuaded Pell to go with her to the judge's office. When they got there, they found the judge was in court. Pell was handed some forms and told to fill out an application. He said he didn't have time right then, that they had some business to attend to, and he marched Helen out of there. He told her, "They will want to know how much education I've had, and you know the answer is *none*."

Helen tried to reason with him, but he wouldn't listen. He insisted that they needed to go shopping. He had her drive him to a furniture store, and he went in and bought an expensive dining room suite—one they didn't need and couldn't afford.

Pell was a highly intelligent man, with a great deal of knowledge in many fields, and he was an expert in the field of law enforcement. But he had very little formal education. He had no problem with self-esteem in South Texas, where his worth and reputation were well-known. But here in the educated, sophisticated atmosphere of the city he felt lost.

Shortly after the experience having to do with the board of pardons position, Pell's brother Clyde and his wife came to visit. When they were ready to go home, they invited Pell to ride back as far as Hebbronville with them, and Helen encouraged him to go. She really didn't know what to do with him in Austin.

He stayed with Ike and Mattie. Ike's health had been poor for the past few years, and Pell could see that it was getting worse. Ike told him he was in pain all the time—said the only thing that helped was a good stiff drink of whiskey: "But Matt waters it down—she pours half of it down the sink and fills the bottle up with water. She'd pour it all down the sink if she had her way."

Pell wrote to Helen and complained bitterly about that: "It's plain damn cruel."

Pell had gone to Hebbronville merely on a visit, but he found a way to prolong his stay. George Holbein, who was the game warden, was drafted into the Army, and he was looking for somebody to take his place, to hold his job for him until he could get back home. Pell

CHAPTER TWELVE

decided to do it. It paid one hundred dollars per month, and it left him quite a bit of leisure time.

They had the Trap leased for grazing, but the lease was about to expire. Pell did not re-lease it. Instead he started building a small house there. It was constructed of hollow tile—one large room with a fireplace. No kitchen, no bathroom, no electricity. The place had a good well that had been there since Mr. Reed used it as a resting place for his cattle. When Pell got the house built, he moved into it.

In Austin, Reginald got a job working at Slaughter's Food Store after school and on Saturdays.

Oil was discovered that fall on the Armstrong ranch, one and one-half miles from the Harbison ranch. Helen and Pell leased their ranch to one of the oil companies for two dollars per acre.

Helen and all the children lived in Austin the rest of that year. But in August, exactly one year after they left the ranch, she brought the three youngest girls and came back to Jim Hogg County and moved into Pell's little house at the Trap. The older children were left in Austin to finish their education. Hazel went to live with Charlie and Margaret Yeoman, whom the Harbisons knew from Hebbronville. Georgia stayed with Mrs. Gill, one of their Austin neighbors. Reginald stayed with other neighbors, the Jones family.

The Trap was the only home available to the Harbisons in the summer of 1943. They had leased their ranch for five years. It would be four more years before they could move back to it.

When Helen got back, she learned the school in Hebbronville was in need of teachers, and that if she could pass a state examination she could have a job. It had been twenty-four years since she forfeited her chance to acquire a permanent teaching certificate when she left teaching to accept the position of county/district clerk.

It was August. Could she review sufficiently to pass that examination before school started? It was one of the biggest challenges she'd faced, so far. She told Pell and the girls she would take time from her books to cook. Everything else was up to them. Alice was twelve, Ida nine, Carrie Lee seven.

Helen studied. She even studied in the car when she and Pell drove to town. With no electricity at the Trap, she studied at night by the light of a kerosene lantern. She passed the examination and started teaching fifth grade in September. She made ninety dollars a month.

Each morning she fixed a pot of beans and a roast with potatoes

With Pell

and other vegetables and left them cooking in the fireplace, for Pell to attend to. At noon she gathered the three girls and drove the two and one-half miles over the unimproved sandy road to the Trap, where Pell had a hot meal waiting for them. Each night she graded papers by lantern light.

Pell bought some brown leghorn chickens and fastened nail-keg nests in the mesquite trees. And he bought a milk cow. After the evening meal, he and Helen would take the girls and go to a field of cane he had planted, and cut cane for the cow. Then they would milk and feed her. They always worked together at it.

One evening when they were cutting cane, the girls became excited. They said there were two rattlesnakes fighting. Helen went to see. To her surprise it was true. The big snakes were coiled close together, with their heads and half of their bodies in the air, striking at each other. She stood and watched, fascinated. Then she became aware of movement at her feet. There was another big rattler, moving slowly away. Pell came and killed the three snakes. They decided that the one Helen almost stepped on was a female and the other two were males fighting over her. "That was the first time we saw rattlesnakes fighting, but it wasn't the last. You don't see it very often, though."

Ike told Helen he wanted to sell Tipperary Farm and put the money into a rent house in town so Mattie would have some income after he was gone. He had the farm leased to the W. W. Jones estate for grazing. Helen helped him sell it to them. He did buy a house in town, and he rented it to a family that had several adult children living at home, including one "that was not right somehow."

The first year Helen and Pell and the three girls lived at the Trap they all lived in that one room. Pell and Helen slept in their big antique bed, the girls slept on the floor, crowded among the living room furniture and the big new dining room suite Pell had bought in Austin. They used a kerosene lantern for light, a cake of ice in a tub for refrigeration. They had bought a new electric refrigerator in Austin, but it was of no use to them now. After a few months they bought a kerosene cookstove.

The family knew that Ike was getting weaker. One afternoon Pell and Helen stopped to see him after she got out of school. On the way home Pell said, "Let's hurry and eat supper and go back in there." They did. And when they arrived Ike was already dead. That was November 10, 1943.

CHAPTER TWELVE

In 1944 Pell added onto the little house at the Trap. He built a kitchen, a bedroom, bath, and screened porch. And he built a storm cellar beside the house. Eventually, they bought a kerosene refrigerator.

In the evenings—after the cow was milked and fed, the eggs gathered, supper over, and the dishes washed—Helen, Pell, and the three little girls often sat in the yard in front of the house and watched the stars. Helen would talk to them about astronomy, and tell them again about the time she saw Halley's comet. Pell usually just sat and listened, smoking Bull Durham cigarettes that he himself rolled. He often had one of the girls on his lap, and sometimes one of them sat on Helen's lap.

Then they would go in the house and Helen would grade papers by lantern light.

Hazel and Reginald stayed in school in Austin, she at the University of Texas and he in high school. But Georgia came back to Hebbronville and lived with Mattie and finished high school there. After she graduated, she worked in the local office of the Texas Company and used her money to pay her expenses at Texas College of Arts and Industries in Kingsville.

One day Mattie told Helen and Pell she would like to go and see Tipperary Farm. "So much of my life was lived there. I just want to look at it again. I want to see the old house."

Shortly after that they took her to Tipperary. They themselves had not been there for a good many years. None of the family had even gone to look at the place when Ike sold it to the Jones estate. Nobody had lived in that general area for a long time. They had to get permission from the Jones family to go there. And when they finally did get to the farm, they all were shocked. The only thing that marked what they believed to be the spot was one lonely hackberry tree. The house was gone, the barn and other buildings were gone, the fences were gone, even the windmill and the pila were gone. There was nothing left to show that any of the farmers who had been enticed to buy land around Santa Rita had ever been there. Santa Rita itself was gone. It was as if the spirit of the prairie had been offended by the intrusion of men who dared to break the land and had magically removed all vestiges of habitation, restoring the spot to its pristine state. If it had not been for the hackberry tree, they would not have found the place.

With Pell

Mattie leaned against the fender of the car. Pell moved to her side. Helen went to examine the tree, to look for the initials Johnny had carved the time he and the Presnalls brought her home after her graduation from high school. She wanted to make sure it was the same tree. It was. The initials were there.

Mattie said, "Gone. All that living. Gone. Not even a trace."

Pell helped her into the car and she slumped against the seat.

Garland and her family lived in Hebbronville, and she saw Mattie every day. The day after the trip to the farm Garland asked Helen, "What's wrong with Mama? She seems so depressed."

Helen told her, and said, "She didn't say two words all the way home."

From that time on Mattie seemed to lose her zest for life. She clung to her independence, but the sparkle, the optimism, the old determination were gone. Many a time they found her just walking back and forth in the yard, keeping her thoughts to herself.

The family in her rent house stopped paying rent. Mattie didn't do anything about it. Her children urged her to order the people to pay or move out. They told her, "Those people have enough money to pay their rent—they have all those big boys working in the oil field."

But Mattie refused to pressure her renters. She said, "I don't want to hound them—they have an afflicted child."

As long as Mattie lived, the people kept on living in her house without paying rent.

In 1945 Reginald finished high school in Austin and came home. He tried to get into the Air Force but was turned down because he did not have 20/20 vision. He then tried to join the Merchant Marines, but they didn't want him because they said he had flat feet. He worked in the oil field for the Texas Company that summer and then was drafted into the Army in the fall—flat feet or no flat feet—and sent to Korea.

Pell stocked the Trap with a few beef cattle, and from the Jones estate he leased some land that he planted in peanuts and cane. The next year Helen persuaded him to rent a piece of land that was across the road from their little house, and plant it in cotton. Just as the bolls were about to open, a government man ordered them to plow it up, as part of a project to control the boll worm. Helen argued with him: "You can't make us plow it up before we pick it. We have to get our money out of it."

He said, "You might as well go ahead and plow it up. Won't do

CHAPTER TWELVE

you any good to pick it—we're closing down the gin; you won't have any place to take it."

They reluctantly plowed up their cotton.

The next thing they knew the gin was reopened. The government man came and told them they had his permission to pick their cotton and have it ginned. Helen was more angry than she could remember ever being. She pointed to the field. "Take a look at that! We did what you ordered us to do!"

The man said, "I see lots of white bolls. You can pick it now."

Helen's hackles rose: "With it mostly plowed under? It's hard enough to find pickers when the cotton is standing up!"

Pell walked up and looked at the man. He didn't say a word—he just looked. The man got in his car and left—quickly.

The government paid them nothing for the cotton it ordered plowed up. They lost everything they put into that crop.

In the spring of 1947 Hazel married Paul Roehr. They were married in Austin. Pell refused to go to the wedding. According to Helen, "He didn't want her to marry—he never wanted any of his daughters to marry."

Alleene and her husband drove to Austin for the wedding and took Helen with them. When Hazel brought Paul home and introduced him to her father, Pell said, "I'm glad to meet my wife's son-in-law."

Mattie was not feeling well that spring. In March Helen wrote to Hazel: "Mama is sick. I wish you'd write to her—it would make her feel better."

On July 1, 1947, the Harbisons moved back to their ranch. In the summer of 1942 Helen had been happy to be leaving it and heading for Austin. Now, five years and many hardships later, she was even happier to be getting back to it.

CHAPTER THIRTEEN

For Helen and Pell, moving back to the ranch was like starting over. Their years at the Trap had not been easy ones. Their standard of living was much reduced from what it was before they moved to Austin, and it would remain reduced for several more years. They had sold their electric generator when they went to Austin. Now, they had no electricity at the ranch. Their laundry facilities consisted of a washboard and galvanized tubs, their lights of kerosene lamps and lanterns. They had to repair the farm machinery and restock the ranch. They went about the comeback gradually, doing most of the work themselves.

They bought a small herd of beef cattle, some of them Brahmas. Pell planted some cotton and cane. Helen planted a garden. Later, they bought a few Jersey cows and started building a dairy herd, doing the milking themselves, by hand.

Mattie died on New Year's Eve, a few months after Helen and Pell moved back to the ranch. Her death did not come as a great surprise. Her children had known for some time that she was not well, and that her will to live was no longer strong. They buried her with sadness, but with peace in their hearts. And life went on.

A year after the Harbisons moved back to the ranch, the Rural Electrification Administration extended service down Randado Road. Now they had electricity for lights, a radio, and a clothes washer. And they bought a milking machine called a Surge. After a cow was milked by the machine, she still had to be stripped by hand, as the machine did not completely empty her udder, but the machine was a big help, nevertheless.

They hired a man to be in charge of the milking, and moved him and his wife and children into one of the tenant houses on the ranch. And they found a man to help with the farming and moved him and his family into the other tenant house. Little by little, life on the ranch

CHAPTER THIRTEEN

returned to something approaching that of the pre-Austin days, except that now Helen and Pell had only three children at home. Hazel was married to Paul Roehr and living in Austin, Georgia was going to college in Kingsville, and Reginald, back from Korea and out of the Army, was attending the University of Texas.

Pell had never wanted Helen or the girls to work in the field, and he had not permitted the girls to ride horses because he feared for their safety. Helen had gone to the cotton field a few times against his wishes, but none of his daughters had disobeyed him. None, that is, until Carrie Lee, who was considered by most people to be "her mother all over again." One day she went to the barn, saddled a horse, and took off into the pasture. The horse ran away with her, but it did not throw her. Pell stood and watched. After that he offered no objection to her riding. She learned to rope, throw, and tie a calf. She was her daddy's tomboy. Soon she was working cattle right along with the hired help.

Their dairy herd was increasing. They were keeping all their Jersey heifer calves, but they removed them from their mothers soon after they were born. When Carrie Lee was twelve, Pell turned the care of the calves over to her. For several years they were her responsibility. She taught them to drink from a bucket, and she fed them morning and evening. "She never lost a calf."

During bad weather in the winters they fed ensilage to the beef cattle as well as to the dairy herd. Ida remembers helping Carrie Lee dig ensilage from the trench silos and carry it in galvanized washtubs and dump it into big cow-feeding troughs. "That ensilage would be warm, and it'd smell *so* good." The big Brahma range cows would push and seem menacing, and Ida was afraid of them. "But Carrie Lee wasn't a bit afraid, she'd hit them on the nose to make them get out of our way."

Alice, Ida, and Carrie Lee rode a school bus to Hebbronville. It picked them up at the gate down by Randado Road, which by now was a blacktop highway. When they came back to the ranch in the afternoons, Helen and Pell would be sitting on the front porch, talking. And smells of hot chocolate and cupcakes would be drifting from the house. Ida recalled: "Mother baked something every day, she had lots of butter and eggs. And when we'd come home, tired and hungry. . . . Oh, those smells would be heavenly."

In 1951 Pell built a new milking barn, with up-to-date equipment, and they started selling whole milk to the Borden Company. They installed electrically cooled storage facilities. The milk, in ten-gallon cans, was picked up by haulers. "You made a lot more money selling whole milk than you did selling cream."

Pell depended upon Helen to do their bookkeeping. He seldom paid attention to that. Usually, he did not even know the status of their checking account. If he needed cash, he went to the bank and wrote a check, and sometimes he overdrew the account. Helen complained to the tellers about that. She said, "Just tell him there isn't enough money in the account."

They told her: "Oh, no! We can't—if we do that Mr. Pell gets awful mad."

The Harbisons nearly always had a radio—before they went to Austin, and after they came back. Before they had REA electricity, they used the radio sparingly—for news, for the Grand Ole Opry on Saturday nights, and for the symphony on Sunday afternoons. They couldn't use it when the generator engine was running because the engine made a lot of noise on the radio, and they didn't want to use it too much when the engine wasn't running because that would run down the batteries. But after they got regular 110/220 volt electricity, they could use the radio as much as they wished. They usually had it on when they were sitting in the living room, or when they were at the dining table.

Pell liked music. And when he was sitting around the house, he liked to listen to it with Helen by his side. He's say, "Miss Helen, you've got big girls to wash the dishes. You come and sit with me." He liked just to sit and listen to music, but Helen liked to read the newspaper, and she was always coming across something she wanted to read aloud to him. When she'd read something he wasn't interested in he'd say, "Damn rubbish!" And when she'd read the obituaries, he'd be exasperated: "God! Can't you find anything more cheerful than that?" When the next paper came, she'd read him the obituaries again.

Once when the three girls came home from school, they found Pell and Helen in the usual place, sitting on the front porch. Pell said, "Go in the living room and see what's in there."

On the mantel sat a baby great horned owl. It had fallen from a nest in a hackberry tree in the yard and Pell had rescued it. They kept it as a pet until it was grown. Carrie Lee caught ground squirrels for its food. It had the run of the house. When it was old enough to take

CHAPTER THIRTEEN

care of itself, they took it to the barn, and it stayed around there for a long time.

Oil companies continued to be interested in drilling in Jim Hogg County. A well was being drilled on the property across the road from the Harbison ranch, and Helen wanted to go and take a look at it. She had maintained a keen interest in the oil business ever since she was county/district clerk during the boom days. Pell wasn't interested in looking at the well. As he and Helen drove to Hebbronville one day, she suggested they drive over to the well site. Pell said no.

But they did. Helen just ignored him. "I was at the wheel, so I just drove over there."

They arrived at a startling moment. The well hit a gas pocket that blew the drilling mud to the top of the derrick and sent the men scrambling for safety. Helen jumped up and down and clapped her hands. Even Pell was excited.

In 1949 Alice graduated from high school and entered the University of Texas.

And on June 1, 1950, Georgia married Vernon Harlan.

With Hazel's experience in mind, Georgia decided to marry at home so her father would be forced to attend her wedding whether he wanted to or not. Pell did reluctantly stay in the living room during the ceremony, but he refused to participate in any way.

Pell was generous in most ways, but he did not wish to share his family with outsiders. He was apprehensive about his daughters' dating, and he was never happy about their marrying. He did not accept his sons-in-law graciously until they had been in the family for some time. Reginald said: "He didn't chew them out, but he didn't go out of his way to be nice, either. Daddy didn't hide any feelings." Perhaps the closest he ever came to showing them he accepted them was once when they were all at home he dropped Helen and the girls off at the soda fountain and took the men to a bar and bought them a drink.

REA electricity was making the Harbison's life somewhat easier. They bought a freezer, and that changed their eating habits. They froze vegetables from Helen's garden and fruit from their trees, and they regularly butchered calves and froze the meat. Beef became more important than pork in their diet. But, in general, things on the ranch had not changed a great deal. Helen and Pell still worked hard.

One day they drove down in one of the pastures to check on a heifer they knew was about ready to calve. When they found her, she was already in trouble. "We saw the calf would have to be taken, so we went for the vet, but he was gone. We came back and got the tractor and a rope, and we went down there and pulled that calf."

They encountered an unusually large number of rattlesnakes one spring. They killed five in one day. Nobody was ever bitten, in spite of the fact that Helen was sure she had stepped on one of the snakes. "I had a setting hen in one hand and a pan of eggs in the other, and I was looking up in the trees at some birds when I heard that familiar rattle at my feet. He was a little fellow, and he was trying his best to get away from me."

The year 1951 was dry. In March, Helen wrote to Hazel: "The mesquite and catclaw are putting out, but it is just pitiful to see how dry and drear the prairies are. The cows try to find something to eat. The wind and sand have blown so today. No doubt we'll get all that sand back from the north tomorrow."

Some men asked permission to set up a rain-making apparatus on the ranch, and they wanted the Harbisons to operate it. Helen wrote to Hazel: "They said they wanted to put it on our ranch because we are close to town, and we have a telephone. They would pay us one dollar per hour for the time we operated it. It is something like a stove. You start it with charcoal, and then use coke, and that separates the silver iodide into trillions of particles. We wouldn't operate it all the time, just when weather conditions were right. They'd call and tell us when."

Pell's reaction was an emphatic No!

"Daddy said we had enough to do without that. And that is true. But if I saw a dollar in something I'd take on a little more."

Helen and Pell went looking for hay or cane to buy for the cows. It was hard to find, because of the drought. They bought one load at Benavides, about twenty miles from the ranch, and made arrangements to go back the next day and get another trailerload. Helen did the driving.

Hazel's husband, Paul Roehr, like Reginald Harbison and many other young men at that time, finished his college education after he came home from the war. When he received his degree, he and Hazel moved from Austin to Dallas. Helen wrote to them: "I hear you are planning to take your cat with you to Dallas. It is bad luck to move a cat."

CHAPTER THIRTEEN

The drought continued until finally Pell was forced to take a torch and burn the spines from the prickly pear plants in the pasture so the cows would have something to eat. Helen wrote to Hazel: "Daddy is sick tonight. He had a bad spell this evening and had to take some medicine. I wish he'd see a doctor but he won't. He has been burning pear every day, and in this heat that gets old."

In 1951 Reginald graduated from the University of Texas with a bachelor of science degree in geology, and Ida graduated from high school and enrolled at the University of Texas, leaving Carrie Lee the only child at home.

In addition to her many duties at the ranch, Helen reviewed Alan Paton's *Cry, the Beloved Country* for the Ladies' Missionary Society of the Methodist Church in Hebbronville. She told Hazel about the book and added: "I'm glad you have joined the Texas Poetry Society. I think you have literary talent, and you should cultivate that talent."

Helen was spending a little more time with one of her own talents —that of cultivating flowers. In March, she had blooming phlox, poppies, anemones, ranunculi, African daisies, stock, asters, larkspur, snapdragons, and lady slippers. She read in the newspaper about a flower show that was to be held in Falfurrias, and she wrote to ask whether she might enter. The answer was yes. As she prepared for it, her excitement rose. A yearning for the beauty expressed in flowers had been in her all her life, but it had been kept subdued most of the time under layers of necessity and practicality. This would be her first flower show.

Two days before the show the temperature soared to over 100 degrees. Helen covered some of her prize flowers with cotton sacks, but even then some of her nicest ones "just cooked." She cut the others and put them in the refrigerator in order to keep them until the show. She had to get them to Falfurrias—a distance of about forty miles from the ranch—before eleven o'clock that morning. Pell went with her.

Part of the road was being repaired, and that slowed them down considerably, so when they reached the end of the construction, Helen stepped down hard on the accelerator, ignoring the speed limit. As they approached a house, two chickens walked calmly into the road. Helen did not alter her speed. Pell yelled at her, "Don't you dare hit those chickens!"

Helen told Hazel, "I'd have run over them if Daddy hadn't been in the car."

As it was, she slammed on the brakes and swerved the car. In the back seat chaos was created—over came the flower containers. Some of the best flowers were broken from their stems. Helen was near tears. She wanted to kill Pell, along with those chickens. She said, "Oh. . . . You and your love of animals!"

They put what was left of the flowers back together and went on to the show. She won a blue ribbon for her asters, a red ribbon for her one lady slipper, and a red ribbon for her phlox.

When they got home, Pell told her to go ahead and order the chain link fence she'd been wanting for her yard and flower garden, to keep out the chickens, guineas, cats, and dogs.

One day when Helen was out by the pila she found two big rattlers fighting. She called Carrie Lee, who came and shot their heads off.

Pell was not feeling well. Helen wrote to Hazel: "Daddy feels terrible. He had a bad spell yesterday. He won't go to the doctor. I wish he would."

In her letters to her children Helen was perpetually concerned with the weather and the oil-drilling situation, both of which constantly either annoyed or excited her. "The drought is still with us. We are selling over $1,000 worth of milk a month, and borrowing money to feed the cows. And the oil company didn't drill, after all, or even ask for a renewed lease. Our oil prospects look dim."

A few weeks later: "We've had rain twice. The pastures are green, the wild flowers are beautiful. A mockingbird is in the hackberry tree, singing at the top of his lungs."

Or: "Humble Oil is interested in leasing our land, so they must think as I do, that the oil vein is under us. They will probably put down a deep well."

In the fall of 1952 Helen voted for Eisenhower. "I was tired of the Democrats and all their controls. And I wanted somebody to get us out of Korea."

On November 21 of that year Alice married Lou Hempel in Austin. Pell refused to go to the wedding.

Helen and Pell sold their beef cattle and put the money into Jerseys for the dairy. It was a well-timed move, because beef prices soon went down.

Christmas night, 1952, Pell became very ill. Several of the children were at home for the holidays. Reginald and Carrie Lee went to Hebbronville for the doctor, and he came back to the ranch with them. He examined Pell and pronounced it a serious heart attack. They real-

CHAPTER THIRTEEN

ized then that those "bad spells" he had been having for the past year or so were probably heart attacks. He was taken off coffee and cigarettes, put on medication, and told to stay quiet for several weeks. Helen learned the technique of caring for him: how to give him nitroglycerin by placing a small pill under his tongue, how to give him meperidine (Demerol) by injection, how to give him oxygen from the portable tank by his bed.

He made at least some effort to cooperate with the doctor, but he was not what could be called a reasonable patient. For one thing, he was not happy unless Helen was by his side, and of course it was impossible for her to be there all the time. In addition to nursing him, she now had to participate to a much greater extent in supervising the operation of the ranch—this on top of an already full schedule of bookkeeping, housekeeping, gardening.

She wrote to her children about the situation: "I want to tell you how much will power Daddy has. He quit coffee and cigarettes, just like that. And you know how much they both meant to him. But he is very impatient. He does not want me out of his sight. I think it would help me to relax if I could get out with my flowers for a while. But there is no chance for that."

CHAPTER FOURTEEN

In the spring of 1953 an oil well was being drilled about a mile southwest of the Harbison ranch. Helen wrote to Alice: "It's so exciting. I wish I could work at the railroad commission office and took at their maps, and see who gets permits to drill where."

Pell sometimes felt better, sometimes worse. Most of the responsibility for the operation of the ranch rested on Helen's shoulders, but she cleared the major decisions with him, no matter how sick he was. From the beginning they had differed in their approach to farming and ranching, and they still did. But it never occurred to her to think of him as anything other than the one in whom the final authority rested, so she adjusted to his decisions. That didn't always come easy. But it came naturally.

By the middle of March she had corn and cane up, and the men were ready to start planting peanuts.

The farming equipment on the Harbison ranch was getting old, and sometimes the farm hands did not handle it carefully. Something was always breaking down, and Helen was always having to go to Hebbronville, or Alice, or Falfurrias for parts. Every day brought emergencies. Sometimes Pell was well enough to go with her, sometimes not.

One day he went with her and Carrie Lee to Laredo to do some shopping and to talk with a Mr. Killam about an oil lease. Helen wrote to Hazel: "I hadn't been up to Laredo in a long time. It made me feel sad. I remembered the time Daddy led the parade, and I got my engagement ring. Daddy was well then. And I remembered when I used to go to Kress's store and buy little things to bring home to you children. All my little children have grown up now, and most of them have flown the coop. We passed Mercy Hospital and I thought about the times I went there to bring home a new baby. Well, that was quite a while ago, wasn't it? I have no babies now. And that reminds me—when am I ever going to get some grandchildren?"

CHAPTER FOURTEEN

In April Pell was "feeling terrible" again. As usual, he would not see a doctor.

They were selling over $1,100 worth of milk a month but barely breaking even.

Helen wrote to her children about a joke she had on Pell. They had a Mexican woman working for them who was about Helen's size and build, so Helen gave her some of her old dresses. One day Pell came in the kitchen and saw a figure in Helen's dress bent over a mop, scrubbing the floor. Being in a playful mood, he gave her a whack on her bottom. To his embarrassment, the face that looked back at him was the maid's, not Helen's. Helen found the incident more than a little amusing, especially in view of Pell's determination to display a very prim and proper demeanor, even in front of the children. She wrote a poem about it:

A Predicament

There was a modest lady
Who had a modest maid;
They were the same in size and figure,
The Mistress and the maid.
The maid was bent in posture
Her meager task to do,
And that is just the reason
Her face was not in view.
When the husband saw the figure
He aimed to play a prank.
Upon his most beloved
He could not resist a spank.
Now he stands in awe and askance;
All excuses seem quite vain,
To make to his beloved
Or to the other dame.

By June of 1953 the rains had not come. The Harbisons were borrowing money to feed their cows. The pastures were dry. Helen wrote to Hazel: "This town is in a terrible fix. The Mexican farm workers have no work as there is no cotton to chop or pick, and the cattlemen and farmers are in a squeeze. Waters Corkill had leased our pasture at the Trap but he is turning it back because the Credit Corporation wouldn't loan him the money to pay his rent."

Carrie Lee was sixteen that summer. She had a friend visiting her

With Pell

at the ranch, and they swam in the pila twice a day, though Helen worried that they might get ear infections. Helen wrote to Alice: "Carrie Lee is so headstrong. She swims in the stagnant water of the pila. She rides as she pleases, any kind of horse. Last week she rode Charro without putting a bridle on him, just a hackamore, and she had on a dress instead of blue jeans. Well, he ran away with her. Her dress got caught behind the saddle, so she had to stay with him. And that she did. I didn't know about it until it was over. Thank goodness, Daddy was asleep and didn't know what was going on. Carrie Lee was pretty shaken up. Her arms and legs were almost black, from where he ran through the brush with her. She was sore all over for several days. I swear to you, sometimes I don't know what to do with that child! She is just terrible. You never know what she will do next."

Alice and her husband, Lou Hempel, were living in Austin, in a veterans' apartment, paying twenty dollars a month rent. He was enrolled at the University of Texas, and Alice was looking for a job. Helen wrote to her with some motherly advice: "You should go to a doctor and be checked over, you probably need some vitamin pills. And you must buy yourself some new clothes before you start being interviewed for jobs."

In the same letter she said the children were not to worry about her and their father. "When Daddy gets up and feels normal again my blood pressure will go down. I believe it has already gone down—I'm leaving off supper these days."

But Helen's children did worry about her and Pell. And they worried about Carrie Lee's being the only child at home to share the burdens. She was a senior in high school, and she was missing a lot of school because Pell was so ill most of the time, and Helen's blood pressure was very high, and there were a lot of errands to run and other things to help with.

Hazel, Georgia, and Alice were married. Reginald was working for the Texas Company in Louisiana. That left Ida, a junior in college, feeling she was the only one who could stop what she was doing and go home to help. And that is what she did. When the fall semester ended, Ida gathered up her things and went to the ranch. She stayed out of school during the spring semester and the first part of the summer term. Only when Pell and Helen were both feeling better did she go back to school.

Helen wrote to Alice and Hazel: "I hate to see Ida stay out of

CHAPTER FOURTEEN

school. But, oh, you don't know how much Daddy wanted her to. He wants every one of you near him."

In spite of all the classes Carrie Lee missed, her semester grades were: journalism 98, civics 94, speech 98, shorthand 92.

There were always a lot of visitors at the ranch, especially on weekends. Helen told Alice: "Daddy still has lots of company. Mr. White and Mr. Dowe, also Mr. McMurrey came the other day. The McGees were back, Myrtle came. Mr. Woods was here again."

In that same letter she said: "I got Pablo to fix another plot for some of my flowers, and he prepared the ground just fine, but he failed to water the plants after he put them out. I think most of them will die. Daddy has a fit if I go into the yard."

Pell kept having what Helen called "nervous spells." Dr. Zec from Hebbronville wanted him to go into the hospital at Laredo, for tests. Pell finally, reluctantly, agreed to go. Garland and her husband, Leuin David, drove them over.

The X rays of Pell's abdomen showed that his large intestine was pushed down by something and that his liver was enlarged. The doctors in Laredo wanted to operate, but Dr. Zec would not allow it because he felt Pell could not live through an operation. So they went home.

The trip to the hospital left Pell weaker than before. Helen said that when they got him back to the ranch and got him to bed "his pulse would race so fast I could scarcely count it, then suddenly slow down and almost stop." She called Dr. Zec and he told her to give him a shot of Demerol. At three o'clock the next morning he woke up hungry, so she fixed him a breakfast of oatmeal, eggs, flour tortillas, and Sanka.

When Pell was in the hospital, his systolic blood pressure was 210 two days in a row, but when Dr. Zec took it the next morning after they got back to the ranch it was 150. That led Helen to believe that the doctors had gotten his problem under control. She told her children: "He has been sleeping and resting all morning. The trip to Laredo was hard on him, but I believe the doctor will get to this trouble of his nervousness. I believe, now, that Daddy will have a chance to live and no doubt be in better health than he has been for a long time."

Hazel was pregnant, expecting her first baby in May, 1954. Helen wrote her: "Be sure and take plenty of exercise. Walking is the best exercise you can get."

In March the dairymen around Hebbronville were having trouble

With Pell

with the Borden Company. Helen wrote to Hazel: "They are sending some of our milk to the cheese factory in Alice, because they say it is off flavor. The cheese factory only pays us $2.08 for ten gallons. We can't produce it for that even when we raise our own feed."

She wrote to the company and told them not to send any more of the Harbison's milk to the cheese factory, just to send it back to the ranch. She told her children: "But it's surplus milk. We don't need it for anything here."

All of the dairymen were having the same trouble. Some of them signed a paper saying that they would withhold their shipments of milk if the Borden Company did not change its policy. The men who signed that paper got a notice from the Borden Company that it would discontinue buying their milk after sixty days. The father of Noé, a young man who worked at the Harbison ranch, was one of the signers. The Harbisons themselves had not signed.

Helen suggested to Noé that perhaps his father could sell his milk to a Mr. Knolle, who was a small independent buyer, and later Noé told her that all those who had signed would change over and sell to Knolle. Helen told her children: "I don't believe we could sell to Knolle, because he advertises that his milk comes from Jerseys only. We have Holsteins as well as Jerseys in our herd." But she vented her annoyance in a letter to the Borden Company. "I wrote them a good one."

Helen had voted for Eisenhower to get rid of some of the Democrats, but she had not gotten rid of all of her problems. She wrote to Hazel: "That old Agriculture Commissioner Benson wants to cut parity on dairy products 15% by April first, and I think that is the seat of our trouble. I wrote to Lyndon Johnson and told him the plight the dairymen would be in if they cut it. I got an answer right back from him, and he said that in the Congress they had introduced a bill, which he thought would pass, to limit any reduction of parity to 5%."

And then there were problems that could not be blamed on the politicians. She wrote to Alice: "You should be here. I have cats running out my ears. Four have had kittens, and two more are expecting. One had hers under the bathtub and we don't know yet how many she had. That ugly mottled cat had five kittens in the cellar. One had hers in a hen's nest, and the old setting hen was so proud of them. One cat's kittens all died—how sad! She was the smoky-blue, long-haired cat. Well, maybe the growing cat population is the answer to our surplus milk problem.

CHAPTER FOURTEEN

It had not rained for some time, and the sand was deep. Ida went to the mailbox on the tractor. She brought back letters from Reginald, Hazel, Alice, and Georgia. Helen said, "It was like a family reunion. I'm glad I have a lot of children."

By April, 1954, Pell was feeling better. He was able to sit up in his chair for several hours each day. His heart was not bothering him much, but he kept having trouble with indigestion.

This was Carrie Lee's senior year in high school. She had been caring for the calves since she was twelve. It kept her tied to the ranch every morning and every evening. Pell decided that she needed to be free from that. He said a young man named Tomás, who was helping with the milking and the farming, would have to take care of the calves. Helen could see that Tomás wasn't happy about that.

Several of the dairymen who were still selling to the Borden Company decided to show up at the plant in Corpus Christi, unannounced, at five o'clock one morning, to taste their own milk at the same time the company's tasters were tasting it. Of course Helen and Pell could not go, so one of the men volunteered to taste the Harbisons' milk for them. They reported, "The Borden men sure were surprised to see us." The man who tasted the Harbisons' milk said it tasted "just fine." But one can was sent back that very day.

Then the Borden Company notified the dairymen that if they would not allow their rejected milk to go to the cheese factory, they would have to pay hauling charges, to Corpus Christi and back. Helen was furious. "They won't even answer my letter."

She wrote to Hazel: "You asked who Knolle was. He owns a big dairy at Sandia, and he has won lots of prizes with his herd, so he opened his own plant at Corpus. Of course he can't compete with Bordens—they have a contract with the government to furnish milk to the air base there."

On April 15, 1954, there was a storm at the ranch. Helen wrote to her children and described it:

> It had been a terrible hot, sultry day, but not many clouds were around. Pell had told Noé and Tomás, who were working in the field, if any dark cloud came up and it got to thundering they should come to the house immediately. I had sent Carrie Lee to town for groceries after she came in from school.
>
> It began to get dark blue in the northwest and southwest, and the clouds began to gather so fast I knew there must be wind in them.

With Pell

Underneath the clouds you could see red, like sand was blowing, but I knew that meant hail this time of the year. When Pell saw the clouds he told me to phone Carrie Lee to come on home. I was lucky in catching her at the store, and before I knew it she was home, but none too soon. The boys just barely made it in from the field before the storm broke.

You can imagine how nervous Daddy was. So I gave him a shot of Demerol. It got dark as night and we had to turn on the lights.

We got everything set to go down in the cellar. In fact, the boys and I took the lead and Ida and Carrie Lee stood by Daddy, but he was afraid it was too cool in the cellar, and he was also afraid he couldn't make it. I kept trying to get him down, holding the lantern so he could see, because by then the electricity had gone off. I knew some big hailstones were falling, I heard them on the outside cellar door. Then I realized Daddy couldn't climb back up those steps if he came down. So I came back up.

A good many of our salt cedars were blown down. Some tin was blown off the roof of the barn, a hackberry tree in front of the old dairy barn was uprooted, as were several mesquites. It did not hail so much at the house, but more fell in the pasture.

Noé had just finished planting the cotton, and he and Tomás were planting cane. The cotton that had already come up got covered with sand.

Helen told Hazel: "The Borden Company has about quit sending milk back." And she told her: "Daddy is asleep now. I'm going to let Ida sit with him while I go water what few flowers I have left. I haven't been able to leave him much lately."

Tomás had been sullen ever since Pell added the care of the calves to his duties. One Sunday evening he came in reeking of alcohol and told Helen he intended to quit if he had to take care of those calves.

Helen was frantic. Tomás was a good worker. Where would she find someone to replace him? She hesitated to tell Pell because she knew it would upset him, and she knew he was in no condition to be upset. But she did tell him. She didn't know anything else to do.

Tomás was single, so Helen served his meals in the kitchen of the ranch house, as she usually did for field hands who had nobody to cook for them. While Tomás was eating breakfast the next morning, Pell got out of bed, "sick as he was," and went to the kitchen. He gripped the back of a chair to steady himself and looked across the table, hard, into Tomás's eyes and said, "How is everything going, Tomás?"

CHAPTER FOURTEEN

Tomás squirmed, and reddened, and stammered, "Okay."

Pell said, "Miss Helen says you are not satisfied."

"I'd had too much beer, Mr. Pell. I apologize. Nothing is wrong."

"You not leaving us?"

"No."

"All right Tomás." Pell went back to bed.

In May, 1954, Hazel had a baby girl and named her Daphne, and Helen and Pell became grandparents for the first time. When Hazel and Paul brought the baby to see them, Pell was so pleased with her that he sent Helen to town to buy clothes and toys for her, and when Helen came back with only two outfits, he sent her back to get more.

By September, Pell was feeling better. Ida and Carrie Lee were both attending the University of Texas—Ida as a second-semester junior, Carrie Lee as a freshman. Now, Helen and Pell were alone at the ranch, except for the hired help.

In June, 1955, Reginald married Beverly Blanchard from Houma, Louisiana. This marriage pleased Pell exceedingly. None of the family ever understood why he accepted his son's marriage so graciously and his daughters' marriages so grudgingly. Helen, also, was pleased with Reginald's marriage. But that was not surprising. She never had any trouble accepting the people her children chose to marry.

In August, Ida graduated from the University of Texas and went to work as a bacteriologist at Texas Children's Hospital in Houston.

Helen and Pell got their first television set that year. Pell, particularly, liked the Perry Como show. And of course they watched the news and the weather reports.

Without the knowledge of her parents, Carrie Lee had been in love with a boy named Robert Anderson while they were in high school in Hebbronville. Now, they were both at the University of Texas, and they wanted to get married. Robert's father was Anglo and his mother was Mexican. Robert wrote to Pell and Helen and told them he realized they might have trouble accepting him, but that he and Carrie Lee loved each other very much, and they wanted to marry.

Helen accepted Robert, and from then on treated him as her own child. Pell had a little difficulty with it. But then, Pell always had difficulty accepting his sons-in-law.

The doctors believed that Pell was taking too much Demerol. He demanded it every time he had trouble with angina, or with nervousness. It relaxed him and calmed him and made him feel better. But the

With Pell

doctors said he was becoming dependent upon it, and they wanted him to stop using it. Helen told them that was not advisable. She believed he needed it. She told them, "If you take it away from him, he will turn to whiskey, and that will kill him."

Dr. Zec said, "Well, I'll dilute some Demerol with water, and you can try that. He won't know the difference."

But Pell did know the difference, and he complained about it. The doctors finally took him completely off Demerol. And, just as Helen predicted, he started drinking whiskey. "Once when he was hurting so bad he drank almost a whole bottle in one day. It worried me so. I should have diluted the whiskey. I wanted to. But I couldn't. I remembered how Pell felt when Mama put water in Papa's whiskey, and I just couldn't do it. But I think the whiskey killed him. He would have been a lot better off with the Demerol, it just relaxed him and eased him."

Carrie Lee and Robert married in the early summer of 1956. They married at the ranch, and Pell sat in the living room during the ceremony, but he wasn't happy about it. After they were married, though, he accepted Robert.

On August 5, 1956, Pell had a massive heart attack, and on August 6 he died. His years of illness had been trying, for him, and for Helen, too. Now the struggle was over.

His funeral procession was the longest anybody in Jim Hogg County had seen, as people from all faiths and all economic stations paid their respects to the man they loved, and feared, but above all respected. Many said that day, "Mr. Pell was the best sheriff we ever had."

Helen went home with a proud heart. A new chapter in her life was about to begin.

Independence, Again

CHAPTER FIFTEEN

Helen was now alone in her ranch house, but she had no time to be lonely. She had a dairy to run, planting and harvesting to supervise, decisions to make. And one thing she needed to put her mind to right away was whether to lease the ranch or keep on operating it. She already had an offer from a man who wanted to lease it.

Helen's friend Mae McCampbell had continued to operate Las Vívoras, the big McCampbell ranch, after her husband Howell died. This was the ranch Howell had inherited from his prominent father, Ralph McCampbell—the ranch where Helen and her sisters had lived one winter and boarded a teacher and attended the little one-room school, the ranch where Helen rode with the cowboys at roundup, where she corresponded with two people she had never seen, where she learned what a Yankee dime was. That was a long time ago. Helen and Mae had not even known each other then. It was before Mae married Howell McCampbell. Now, Howell had been dead for more than ten years, and Mae had operated Las Vívoras by herself all that time. Helen decided, "If Mae can, I can."

To a large extent the everyday operation of the Harbison ranch had rested on Helen's shoulders ever since Pell's first heart attack. But now the whole responsibility would be hers. It was a good thing she liked challenges, because she was about to face plenty of them. For one thing, when Pell died they owed nearly $20,000 at the bank. A combination of unfavorable weather conditions, inadequate attention to the operations of the ranch during Pell's illness, and big doctor and hospital bills with no medical insurance had forced them to keep borrowing money. To attain solvency would not be easy. But nothing seemed impossible to Helen. She vowed she would make her ranch produce, and that she would bring her financial situation under control.

She set up a conference with her lawyer—important South Texas

Independence, Again

attorney Jacob Floyd—and with her banker, to discuss ways of handling her debt.

She assessed her farming operations and began planning. Without Pell to restrain her, she could now plow up whatever amount of land she felt she needed. She decided to experiment with different kinds of field crops.

Then she turned her attention to her dairy. Tomás was not pleasing her, so she let him go. She replaced him with José Suarez, a man with a wife and several children. It turned out to be a wise move. José operated her dairy from then on, for as long as she had a dairy. José operated it, but Helen herself supervised it. She made all the decisions: what kind of feed to use and how much, when to dry up a cow, which cows to sell. She named each of her dairy dows and each heifer calf. She knew them by name when she saw them in the barn or in the field, and she kept accurate and detailed records on each one.

The dairymen in that area had been shipping milk in ten-gallon cans, but the Borden Company to whom the milk was being sold requested that all producers install electrically cooled storage tanks, where the milk could be kept until the haulers picked it up and transported it in tank trucks. A man named Cotton Clark had hauled the Harbisons' milk for years, even before they moved to Austin, and had allowed their children to ride the milk truck to town in the days before there was a school-bus route down Randado Road. He had always been a good friend. He told Helen he thought none of the haulers would be hauling milk in cans much longer, that they were switching to tank trucks, that he himself would be switching soon. So she got a 250-gallon stainless steel tank and installed it in the milk room at the barn. Now, all the hauler had to do was drive up to that tank and use a hose to suck the milk into the refrigerated tank on his truck.

José was a good worker. The dairy began to show a profit. Helen decided to sell the range cattle she had at the Trap and put the money into dairy cows. She heard about a good herd of Holsteins in Wisconsin, and she telephoned and bought twelve springer heifers—young cows that had been bred but had never had a calf. "I knew if I bought heifers I wouldn't be getting a cow somebody was dumping because she had a bad udder." The heifers proved so satisfactory that she later bought twelve more.

Helen began attending all functions at the Methodist Church, and she joined the Cenizo Garden Club and immediately took an active part.

CHAPTER FIFTEEN

The four Sewell sisters, c. 1960. *Left to right:* Alleene, Opal, Garland, and Helen. *Below:* Helen, with grandchildren Jennifer, Robert Clyde, and Meredith, c. 1965.

Independence, Again

Helen Sewell Harbison, c. 1975.

CHAPTER FIFTEEN

Helen with some of her flowers in her den.

Independence, Again

The garden club took its name from a shrub called cenizo—*Leucophyllum frutescens* (Berland)—common in South Texas and Mexico, that is covered intermittently from June to September with flowers ranging from white through pink to purple. The way the plant itself came by the name cenizo is explained in a legend that Helen found delightful. It was told by J. Frank Dobie in *Texas and Southwestern Lore* (p. 9):

> It had been an unusually hard winter, cold and dry. . . . Spring came, and with it new hope. But whatever young, green things sprang up died for need of water. The mesquites were mere ghosts; the huisaches, shameful of not bearing their sweet-smelling velvety blooms, hid their leaves. All the waterholes had dried up, and death and starvation ruled the prairie. . . .
>
> There was just one possible way of salvation, and that was prayer, prayer to the Virgin. The cowmen gathered together and reverently knelt on the plain to beg for help. As the last prayer of the rosary was said, a soft breeze, a *lagueño* blew from the east. Soon drops began to fall; all night the rain fell like a benediction.
>
> Filled with new hope, the people rose early the next day to see the blessing that had fallen over the land. . . . As far as the eye could see, the plain was covered with silvery shrubs, sparkling with raindrops and covered with flowers, pink, lavender, and white.
>
> It was a gift of the Virgin, and because the day was Ash Wednesday the shrub was called *el cenizo* (ashes).

In May, 1957, Carrie Lee and Robert's first child—Robert Clyde—was born. Finally, Helen was accumulating a few grandchildren: Hazel's Daphne was three years old, Georgia's Cynthia was one, and now there was baby Robert Clyde. Being a grandmother delighted her.

Another thing that delighted her was the way José Suarez was taking care of her dairy. She built for him and his family a new cinderblock house with electricity, hot and cold running water, and all modern conveniences.

Also in 1957, Helen's sister Alleene lost her husband and Helen invited her to come and live at the ranch. All of the Sewell siblings were still living at that time. Garland and her husband, Leuin David, were living in Hebbronville; Opal, who had been a widow for several years, was teaching school in the Houston area; Emil was still in the asylum at San Antonio; Harold was farming in Jim Hogg County and had never married; and Howard and his wife Covie were living at Orchard, Texas, where he was working for the Duval Sulphur Company.

CHAPTER FIFTEEN

Watermelons were being grown as a commercial crop in Jim Hogg County in 1957, and Helen decided to try her hand at that. She put in about twenty acres, and she got a good crop. But she had the same problem with her melons that her parents had with their onions when Helen was a child—she couldn't find a market for them. The big commercial watermelon growers were selling their melons through exclusive brokers, who bought them by the trainloads. Nobody was interested in Helen's relatively small field of melons. She wrote to Hazel: "I failed completely with my watermelons, but I made a come back in another way regarding melons. I turned my cows in the watermelon patch and that brought milk production up."

She decided to get out of the watermelon business herself, but Jim Hogg County was watermelon country in the early 1960s. Each year Hebbronville selected a watermelon queen and celebrated with a festival. Helen leased 90 acres of the ranch to a man named Wolverton and 300 acres of the Trap to a Mr. Cattles from Falfurrias, both of whom planned to raise melons. Mr. Cattles promised to clear the brush from the 300 acres and pay her five dollars an acre rent. That was about twice as much as she had been getting for the house and pasture at the Trap. She told Hazel: "After he gets through with it the brush will be gone and I can plant buffel grass and graze two or three times as many cattle as I've been grazing. I think that is very good." The fierce competitiveness that characterized Helen when she was younger was still with her. She enjoyed winning.

At a social gathering in Hebbronville she noticed a man she had not seen for many years. She walked up and said, "Do you know who I am?" The man didn't know her. She said, "I'm Helen Sewell Harbison."

"Well I'll be damned!" said the man. "You and I ran against each other for county/district clerk, way back there in the early twenties."

"Yes, and I beat you!" said Helen, with an impish grin.

In August of that year Helen's fourth grandchild—Paul Bruce Roehr —was born. She wrote to Hazel with some advice about how to keep three-year-old Daphne from being jealous: "Make sure she realizes that he belongs to her, too."

Helen was enjoying having a free hand to experiment with farming. And, although her ideas did not always work out as she hoped, on the whole she was successful. She wrote to her children in September, 1957 that she had cut the note down at the bank from $19,585.01 to $15,485.01 since January 31.

Independence, Again

In 1959 Helen's children were scattered here and there across Texas and Louisiana. Ida had been working as a bacteriologist at Texas Children's Hospital in Houston ever since she graduated from the University of Texas in 1955. In January, 1959, she married William Luttrell and continued to work and live in Houston.

Carrie Lee and Robert were both attending the University of Texas, and they and their children were living in Austin.

Hazel and Paul and their two children were living in Dallas. Paul was an executive at one of the banks and Hazel was teaching.

Alice and Lou were living in Corpus Christi.

Georgia and Vernon and their three-year-old Cynthia were in Ozona.

Reginald was working as a geophysicist, and he and Beverly were living in Metairie, Louisiana.

Helen had begged for grandchildren for years before she got any. Now she began to be bombarded with them. From 1954 to 1957 she accumulated four. Then Carrie Lee had Jennifer in 1958 and Meredith in 1960. Ida had Bob in 1959, and Georgia had Martin in 1961. That made eight grandchildren in seven years.

Things were running smoothly at the ranch. She had bought another tractor and hired another farm hand. The dairy was doing well. José was milking a hundred cows and getting more milk than the cooling tank would hold, so she bought an additional tank, a 300-gallon one. In June, 1961, she was in high spirits again. She had gotten two rains at the ranch and her crops and pasture were in good shape.

And she had another reason for being pleased. Through a mistake, Carrie Lee's grade report was mailed to the ranch instead of to her Austin address. Helen opened the envelope. She told Alice: "I couldn't resist looking at them. I'm so proud of her! She made four B's and one A. I think that is wonderful when you consider it's from the University of Texas, and she has three children and a husband and a home to look after."

Anytime Reginald or one of the sons-in-law was at the ranch he worked—plowing, cultivating, harvesting, filling the silos. In July, Helen wrote again to Alice: "It's noisy around here. The bulldozer is root plowing [digging mesquite brush up by the roots], and Bubs and Merdado are filling the silo. Then I have a boy working on the garden fence."

Helen kept things moving.

In that same letter she told Alice: "My night blooming cereus had

CHAPTER FIFTEEN

two blooms the other night! They stayed open until after eight o'clock. I took a whole roll of pictures."

A man approached her about buying the Trap. He offered seventy-five dollars per acre for it. She turned him down. Afterwards, she asked her children's opinion about it.

In addition to managing the ranch and her flower garden, and keeping up with her family, she tried not to miss anything important that was going on in the world. She always watched the evening news on television. On July 21 she wrote to her children, "I presume you saw the second astronaut go up in space."

In October of that year Helen, Garland, and Leuin were all three in Temple, Texas. Helen and Leuin were both at Scott and White Hospital. She was undergoing tests and having a general physical; he was having an operation for cancer. Helen wrote reassuringly to Hazel: "I think I had a very good report. I have no gall bladder trouble which I thought I had, I have no sugar in my blood, nor any other disease. I do have high blood pressure 210/110 and that has caused my heart to be a little enlarged, and I have a diaphragmatic hernia but the doctor has instructed me to sleep with my head higher than my feet, and not to lie down two hours after eating."

After she went home she wrote again to Hazel: "The cane Paul broke the ground for when you were down here is ready to cut now." And she told her: "A norther is here. You can feel the grit on this letter. It's blowing all the caliche off my new road."

She was pleased with the way her dairy was going. Milk production was up. José was a conscientious worker. And he had a nice family. Helen's chief concern about him—and a thing she sometimes counseled him about—was that he and María and their children spent too much of his salary at the bingo tables in Realitos (there were no bingo games in Hebbronville). But in most ways she was well satisfied with the Suarezes.

On the other hand, she was not so happy with the men who worked her fields. She was having difficulty finding reliable farm hands. She believed that two different ones had stolen and butchered calves that belonged to her. And once, when it seemed to her that one of her farmers was not getting the work done as fast as he should, she got on a tractor and rode out to the field and found the man asleep in the shade of his tractor. "They think they can get away with things like that when they work for a woman. He didn't expect me to come out there to check on him."

Independence, Again

Some of the men she hired had never driven mechanized farm equipment, and they didn't know how to take care of it. They ran on flat tires and ruined them; they burned up engines; they broke things. One backed a truck too close to the edge of a silo and upended it into the silo. Helen got rid of him.

One man she dismissed tried to set fire to one of her tenant houses before he left the ranch. She went to the house after he had gone and found a pile of rags smoldering on the kitchen floor.

The young couple she hired to replace the arsonist got into a fight and the sheriff came to the ranch. Helen wrote to Ida, "I really appreciate José when I compare him with these last two."

Helen was sixty-five years old, but she had not slowed down. She was always up by four o'clock in the morning, writing letters, keeping records. December 7 she wrote to Alice: "I know if I get any Christmas cards written it will be before day light, because I'm gone when it's light—mainly to the yard." Almost every afternoon she was going to parties or meetings. "A shower was given Bill Hellen's wife at the Jones Building Tuesday. And yesterday the ladies of the Episcopal Church had a tea out at Mae McCampbell's ranch. I went and took Garland, Estelle East and Margie Robertson. There was many a person out there. Every thing looked so Christmasy. I just love that ranch. It brings back so many fond memories."

There were lots of quail around the ranch that December. Helen heard them calling in the pasture in front of the house, and she saw a big covey down behind the dairy barn. She told Alice she wished Lou were there. "My old gun stock is broken, and my gun kicks so I don't care whether I shoot or not."

Carrie Lee wrote to Helen and said Meredith was turning into "a real pill," that she would "tackle anyone that crosses her." She said the baby-sitter told them Meredith dumped a big boy out on his head when he got in the wagon she was pulling. Helen wrote back and said, "Like mother, like daughter." If Helen's mother had been there she would probably have said, "Like grandmother, like granddaughter."

Helen wrote to Hazel: "I talked with Alice on the phone yesterday and she told me you hadn't been feeling too well. You just better slow down and take care of yourself or your health will break down completely. Good health is one of the main assets for happiness. How much time does teaching involve? Does it make you nervous?"

Helen felt responsible not only for her own children but also for

CHAPTER FIFTEEN

her employees and their families. María Suarez was expecting a baby, and it was Helen who took her to Hebbronville when her labor pains started. The doctor had a delivery room in conjunction with his office, and that is where he installed María.

Helen could see that María was anxious in this unfamiliar place. She was torn between staying with her and going back to the ranch. It was now four o'clock in the afternoon. Helen was to be hostess to the Women's Society of Christian Service at nine o'clock the next morning, and she needed to make some cookies and arrange some flowers. Also, María's family needed to be fed and looked after—José couldn't do it; he had to be at the dairy barn from three every afternoon until nine or ten o'clock at night.

The doctor examined María and said he didn't think the baby would be born until sometime after midnight, so Helen decided to go home. She told María the doctor and nurse would take good care of her, that she herself would be back as soon as she fixed supper and saw about things at the ranch.

It was after seven o'clock when Helen got back to town. The doctor's office was in the old Stroman building, upstairs over the Piggly-Wiggly store, and the stairway that went up there had a door at the street level. When Helen got there the door was locked. She pounded on the door and yelled, but she got no response. She was upset, but not as upset as she was going to be in a few minutes.

She went to Garland's house and called the doctor's office—to tell them to come down and unlock that door and let her in. The telephone rang and rang, but nobody answered. Helen couldn't believe it. Was María up there all by herself? She tried to call the doctor's home but kept getting busy signals. Finally she tried the home of the doctor's nurse, and got her. She said she had locked the door and gone to eat supper; she'd come right over to the office. She came, but she could not get the door unlocked. By this time Helen was frantic. The nurse ran to the service station and called the doctor, and he hurried over, but he couldn't get the door unlocked, either. Helen began expressing her concern in a voice that was not overly conciliatory. The doctor kicked the door down, breaking glass all over the place, and he and the nurse ran up the stairs so fast that Helen couldn't keep up with them, and went into María's room and closed the door. Helen heard him tell the nurse, "We'll have to give her a shot to quiet her."

Helen opened the door and "just marched in there." The doctor

Independence, Again

said the baby would not be born until three o'clock the next morning. Helen said, "I think it's coming 'way before that." The doctor said it wasn't, and he and the nurse went home, leaving Helen in charge.

María was calm now, probably because of whatever was in that shot they had given her, but she said she was hungry. Helen decided to leave her long enough to go to Garland's house and get some chicken soup, and María did eat some of it. Then they discovered they had another problem: they couldn't get into the bathroom—it was locked. "Well. Boy! Howdy! There I was—with a woman about to have a baby, and no bathroom." María's pains were coming close together now. "I didn't even have a time piece, but I know to count to sixty makes about a minute, and she was having pains every minute and a half. I said to myself—I don't care what that doctor said about that baby coming at 3 A.M., it wasn't going to wait—so I phoned him to get down there."

When he examined María, he told Helen, "Phone my nurse and tell her to get here immediately—this baby is almost here."

Helen said, "I told you so," and went to the telephone.

Until the nurse arrived, Helen had to help the doctor. "I was shaking all over—partly because I was mad, and partly because I was scared."

At ten o'clock the baby was born—an eight-and-one-half-pound boy—"so cute and fat."

The doctor wanted to keep María there overnight, and he wanted Helen to stay with her. But Helen had other ideas. A norther had blown in. And there wasn't any heat in that old building at night. "Besides, I knew if María needed something in the night I'd have a fat chance of getting the doctor down there. I told him I thought I'd better take her to the ranch, that we could take better care of her and the baby at home."

"He said, 'All right.'

"I think he was glad to get rid of us."

José and María had made arrangements for María's aunt to come and stay with them for a few days after the baby was born. By the time Helen stopped to pick her up and they all got to the ranch, it was long past midnight. Even that late, "I couldn't sleep until I took 2 high blood pressure pills and 2 aspirins."

The next morning, after she made sure María and the baby were all right, Helen took cookies and coffee and flowers and went to Hebbronville to the Women's Society of Christian Service meeting.

CHAPTER SIXTEEN

In January, 1962, South Texas experienced some very cold weather. The temperature was thirteen degrees above zero Fahrenheit at the ranch. Everything froze. The milk pump and tanks froze. The water lines froze. The fruit trees were killed. Helen saved a bushel of oranges by having them picked when she heard the weather forecast. But lemons, grapefruit, and the rest of the oranges froze on the trees.

The weather usually kept Helen in a state of either euphoria or depression, but she had learned to cope with that as she had with other things. She had learned to balance in her mind those things that were frustrating with things that brought her satisfaction and joy. And now, she was soon to learn of something that would lift her spirits. In February, Reginald went to work for the U.S. Department of Commerce, in the U.S. Coast and Geodetic Survey's Oceanographic Analysis branch. His mother was proud and very pleased.

As large a factor as the weather was, it wasn't the only thing to contend with. In June, 1962, Helen declared that her dairy was "getting to be a bigger headache each day." Although her cows were giving lots of milk, it was selling for only about half as much as it had been selling for when she and Pell built the new barn eleven years before. In addition to that, she was paying more for the feed she bought. She told Hazel that some months she was barely breaking even.

But she found some things to be pleased about. She had gotten two and a half inches of rain. Mr. Cattles had a bumper crop of watermelons at the Trap, and Mr. Wolverton had been harvesting melons at the ranch for over two weeks, sometimes as many as four trailer loads a day. "And those trailers hold 30,000 pounds."

Hebbronville was planning a watermelon festival for June 16. Helen looked forward to the parade and the crowning of the queen.

Earnest Armstrong and his wife, Edith, were Helen's neighbors

Independence, Again

now, living at El Sordo, the old E. L. Armstrong ranch. They had remodeled the stone house, adding to it and making it into a beautiful modern home. In the afternoon before the watermelon festival they planned a punch party in honor of one of their nieces who was to be married soon. Garland and her friend Bessie Mattox were coming out to go with Helen. And that started Helen remembering the many times she and her friends had been entertained at El Sordo when she was young. "Mr. and Mrs. Armstrong were such wonderful hosts. We rode horses, swam in the pila, played games, sang. And I usually gave recitations. There was always so much food—lard cans full of cookies and tamales, lots of pies and cakes. Earnest was just a baby then. I used to carry him around."

By July Helen's crops were in need of rain. She wrote to Hazel, "We have not had any rain in over a month and the pasture is parched." The rains she got in June produced good feed, though. "I do have one silo almost full and have enough big cane to fill the other if it doesn't burn up before I can cut it." It was an eternal gamble—would she get rain when she needed it, or wouldn't she?

The last of July she went to Houston to visit Ida and Bill. She wrote to Hazel and described that visit. She said they took her out to eat in a "very exclusive" place called the Green Parrot. "It was once an old mansion. It is set back from the street with a yard of huge trees and pretty lawn and overlooks a beautiful garden in the back—which, of course, attracted my eye—a fountain with bubbles blowing, Magnolia trees, Mimosa trees and tall, tall trees, low shrubs, and caladiums and flowers."

They also took her to the zoo. "There was a new building which cost $186,000.00. In it, the main attraction to me was the orchid garden, which was a sunken garden sprayed with mist, and artificial trees upon which grew real orchids."

And they took her to the recently completed Sharpstown Mall. "That was something new to me—where all stores are under a glass roof and it is all air-conditioned."

In August some of her children were at the ranch to celebrate Helen's birthday. "While Robert was here he cleaned and mowed my yard and took down that back fence."

Vernon and Georgia were getting ready to move to Waco, where he would begin a Ph.D. program at Baylor University, and Georgia would teach at Connally Air Base.

CHAPTER SIXTEEN

Helen continued to have trouble with her farm hands. She told her children: "Well, I fired Erasmo this week. He got to drinking and running on flat tires and he liked to have ruined all my tires and broke up my ensilage cutter. I had to buy $126.00 worth of parts, mainly because he wouldn't tighten bolts. The other day I told him to put the go-devil on to clean out some little cane and he deliberately ignored me and used the cultivator, so when he came in from the field I fired him."

Now, she had the job of finding a new farmhand.

In August, 1962, Reginald was on the U.S. Coast and Geodetic Survey ship *Explorer* in the Gulf of Maine. He told his mother, "We plow the ocean night and day making depth, seismic reflection, and magnetic profiles in the same way you would plow a field—except our rows are a mile apart." He told her Longfellow's home was in Portland, that it was well kept and new looking, as were all the other homes there.

Helen was delighted with Reginald's interesting experiences, and the things he told her about historic Portland. She said, "I wish I could go up there and see that place."

On August 25 she wrote to Hazel: "Myrtle Draper's brother, Eugene Holman, died. You know he was once president of the Standard of New Jersey. Myrtle flew to New York for the funeral."

And she told her: "I received one inch of rain right on my cane where I needed it."

But by September she was crying for rain again. "It looks like rain and then goes and rains on some other ranch."

And she kept on having trouble with the farm equipment. "I am so sick of that ensilage cutter. It keeps me busy running to Falfurrias getting parts. I've been out about $250.00 on it and it's still breaking down. Sometimes I contemplate selling out and quit worrying, then I can go more."

In October she got almost six inches of rain in less than two weeks. Once it came down so fast it ran into the house and the dairy barn.

Also in October she started having trouble with the Coastal Bend Milk Producers Association, the cooperative to which the producers in her area belonged, which sold milk to the Borden Company in Corpus Christi, and through which payment for the milk was channeled back to the producers.

The association wanted to take over the hauling of milk itself and

Independence, Again

shut out the men who had been doing the hauling. One of the haulers was Cotton Clark, who was Helen's friend who had hauled the Harbison's milk for more than twenty years. Cotton did not want to give up his route, so he got Jacob Floyd, the popular South Texas lawyer, to draw up a petition, and he asked the people on his route to sign it. The petition said its signers would resign from the Coastal Bend Milk Producers Association if they took Cotton Clark's route away from him. Helen signed. The president, vice-president, and one of the directors of the association came and talked with her, trying to convince her she had been wrong to sign the petition. She said she was sticking by Cotton. They said the association intended to take over the hauling of her milk, that there was nothing she could do about it. She told them, "We'll see about that."

She padlocked her gate. The association did not force the issue. Cotton continued to haul her milk.

But Helen went to Premont to attend a Jersey dispersal sale, to learn how it was conducted, to see what the cows brought—just in case the association pushed and she decided to sell her herd. She knew she had not heard the last of them.

October 18, 1962, Ida and Bill called to say that their second child had arrived and that they called her Anne. They didn't mention a middle name. The next day Helen wrote to them and said that she and Alleene, who was still living at the ranch, had spent all evening thinking up names for the baby: "I thought of a pretty name and one which would go well with Luttrell. It is Letticia. Don't you think Letticia Ann Luttrell would be pretty?"

Ida wrote back and said the baby's name was Anne Margaret.

Alleene spent several days in Corpus Christi that fall, being treated for skin cancer. She stayed with Alice and Lou. Helen and Myrtle Draper drove down to get her when she was well enough to come back to the ranch. Helen later said she had been somewhat apprehensive about driving in the city. "It was the first time I ever drove right down in Corpus, but it was nothing."

That fall a preacher came to the ranch to talk with Alleene about buying into a retirement home called Wesley Manor that was being built at Weslaco, Texas. Alleene was determined to move into some place that offered nursing care, because she did not want to be a burden to any of her relatives if she should come down with a lingering illness, so it was easy for the preacher from Weslaco to recruit her for

CHAPTER SIXTEEN

his project. He turned from Alleene to Helen and said, "Mrs. Harbison, why don't you sell your ranch and invest the money in a nice apartment in Wesley Manor, where you would not have any cares or worries?"

Helen looked straight at him for a few seconds. "I'd just as soon go to the penitentiary," she told him.

On October 20 she told Ida that the army worms had eaten up all the grass in her pasture. She said they were starting to eat her cane now, and that she was having it cut, although it was not yet ripe. "I want to beat them to it."

October was the month for planting bulbs, but Helen complained that she had been "running around so much" she was behind with some of her planting. She told Ida she had already planted Dutch irises, Easter lilies, alliums, stars of Bethlehem, and King Alfred daffodils. She said she planned to plant some ranunculuses and anemones immediately, and then to plant more of each in November, as she wanted them to bloom late for the Cenizo Garden Club flower show. She was squeezing the care of her flowers in between all her many other enterprises. She had a deep respect and love for flowers, and a great need for them.

November 12, 1962 — a little more than six years after Pell died — Helen wrote to her children regarding her financial situation: "I still owe the bank some money, but I can now see my way out. In six years I have paid in $14,053.15 on the principal and almost $4500.00 on interest." She told them that in addition to that she had built a $3,000 house for José and his family, had bought a tractor, a trailer, and an ensilage cutter, had dug two big silos, had gotten 616 acres cleared of brush, and had done "a lot of cross fencing." She went on to tell them: "I believe by this time next year, the Lord willing, I can finish paying off my debt at the bank. It will certainly be a good feeling to get out of debt."

The Coastal Bend Milk Producers Association was still making trouble for Helen and the others who signed the petition. They started holding out part of the money due producers, for what they called "damages," for the inconvenience caused when producers objected to the association's taking over the haulers' routes. The check Helen received for November had $247.75 taken out of it. Jacob Floyd went to court and got an injunction to keep the Borden Company from paying the producers through the association, ordering it to pay the producers direct. The association went to court itself and asked that the injunction be reversed. A hearing was held in Alice on January 2, 1963, and Helen

Independence, Again

drove the fifty-three miles to Alice, by herself. It was nine o'clock that night when it was over, and ten-thirty when Helen got home. Alleene, Garland, and Georgia were worried about her and had been telephoning people in Alice to try to learn what had happened to her. She told them, "I wouldn't have missed being there for anything—as at the close of it, Jake Floyd got up and expounded. I never heard such oratory in my life. He told the Coastal Bend just what they were."

The judge decided that the order to restrain the Borden Company from paying the producers through Coastal Bend would remain in effect, and that Coastal Bend must give back to the producers the money they had withheld. When it was over, Jacob Floyd escorted Helen out of the courthouse and to her car. He said, "I gave them hell, didn't I?"

At the end of January Helen got her $247.75 back from the Coastal Bend Association. After the association lost at the hearing in Alice, it took the case to the court of appeals in San Antonio, and the judge there decided in favor of the producers. He refused to revoke the restraining order, and he ordered Coastal Bend to give back the money it had withheld. But that hearing was concerned with the restraining order and the withholding of funds only—the main trial would be held later.

Garland's husband, Leuin David, died, and Alleene left Helen's ranch and went to live in Hebbronville with Garland, because she believed Garland now needed her.

Reginald and Beverly were living in the Washington, D.C., area, where he was helping to process the data he and the others had gathered while on the ship during the summer. Helen knew he was also taking a correspondence course from the University of Texas.

The milk producers finally won in their battle with the Coastal Bend Milk Producers Association. When it was all settled, Helen received $102 as her share of what they claimed the association owed them.

Sometime in the spring or early summer of 1964 Helen hired a new farm hand. His name was Jesús Gonzales. He and his wife Rosa moved into one of the tenant houses. They had no children. Each had children by a former marriage, but the children were not living with them. Helen knew she liked the appearance of Jesús and Rosa. But none of them knew then that this was the beginning of a warm and long-lasting relationship.

Carrie Lee completed her work at the University of Texas that spring and took a job teaching in Hebbronville. She and Robert moved from

CHAPTER SIXTEEN

Austin to the Trap. Because his education had been interrupted by a stint in the armed forces, he was not yet through school. He planned to go back to Austin in September to finish. He worked with Jesús the rest of the summer, cutting feed and filling silos.

During the summer of 1964 Reginald and other scientists participated in the International Indian Ocean Expedition on the U.S. Coast and Geodetic Survey ship *Pioneer*. The expedition was done in cooperation with United Nations Educational, Scientific, and Cultural Organization (UNESCO). They traced a rift valley from Indonesia through the Andaman Sea into Burma.

In November, Reginald was awarded U.S. Patent No. 3116559 for a seismic dip plotter and migrator that he had independently invented.

Also in November, Alice and Lou Hempel took Helen to California for a vacation. "We visited the Redwood National Park. Snow had already covered the tops of the mountains. The huge trees were awesome. The sound of one's voice would cause the snow to start falling off the trees. Alice shoveled snow away to make a path to the Sherman tree."

January 10, 1965, Ida and Bill Luttrell called Helen to say their third child, and Helen's eleventh grandchild, had arrived. They named him William, Jr., and immediately started calling him Billy.

Carrie Lee was pregnant, and she was having trouble with swelling of her body. Helen was concerned and tried to get her to stop teaching, but she felt Carrie Lee would be all right after the baby was born.

On April 19 Robert and Carrie Lee went to Falfurrias to see a doctor, leaving the three children—Robert Clyde, Jennifer, and Meredith—with Helen. The day started off hot and humid. Helen said she had a feeling a storm was brewing. "The weatherman didn't predict anything, but the yellow headed cow birds were here and they always come a day ahead of rain."

About three o'clock it began clouding up. When the lightning and thunder started, Helen got on a tractor and hurried to the field and told Jesús to come in. José was getting ready to milk. He and Jesús decided to take their families to the barn and wait out the storm in the well-protected feed room.

The clouds were puffy. Those in the north were pink.

A constable named Gonzales and his wife stopped by the ranch as the storm was gathering, and Helen invited them to come in the house until it was over. Mrs. Gonzales did, but the constable got caught at the barn.

Independence, Again

This was not going to be a mild storm. Helen could see the red sand coming, high as the sky, from the northwest. It was moving in fast. She began closing windows and doors. Even with the house closed, the air inside got so full of sand that breathing was difficult.

The north door blew open, and Helen looked for a hammer to nail it shut. The children ran screaming from the bedroom. Mrs. Gonzales gasped for breath. Windows were breaking. In one of the bedrooms a big piece of lumber was lying across the bed; it had blown in through the window.

It got dark as night. Helen grabbed a flashlight and pushed the children toward the cellar, urging Mrs. Gonzales to come also. The cellar steps were full of boxes and other things. Helen began kicking them down. Some of the children were crying. Mrs. Gonzales was vomiting. Finally they were down in the cellar. Meredith didn't like being there. She insisted she had to go to the bathroom. Helen told her, "Either hold it or go squat in the corner." They could hear the hail pounding the outside cellar door. They could feel the wind blowing through the house above, but that wasn't Helen's chief concern. "I was thinking about Carrie Lee and Robert."

When it was over and they went upstairs, they found broken glass and water everywhere. All the windows on the north side, and four on the west side, were out. A huge hackberry in the front yard was uprooted. The garage was blown to pieces and debris was all over the yard. No trees had any leaves on them. The pasture, where earlier that day there had been grass and wild flowers, was completely bare. All the crops were gone. Hail covered the ground, two or three feet deep in the corner of the yard. But Pell's concrete house was standing, solid as ever. It had just withstood a tornado.

Carrie Lee and Robert came home. They had driven through rain but they had not been caught in the tornado. They said they had come by the Trap and had found practically no damage there. It was not until they approached the ranch that they realized there had been a bad storm. Prickly pear cactus had been beaten to a pulp, the ground was bare, and water ran like a river through Helen's fields. When they got to where they could see the devastation around the ranch house, they thought everybody had been killed. "They just grabbed their children and cried, they were so glad to find them alive."

During the storm the dairy cows had broken through the fence and tried to find shelter among the salt cedars behind the house, but that

CHAPTER SIXTEEN

had afforded them little protection from the hail. They had bloody spots on their backs and sides. There was no electricity at the ranch until the next day, and some of the cows got mastitis because they could not be milked when the electric milking machines did not work. The storm caught Helen with her silos empty because she could ordinarily expect to have plenty of pasture at this time of year. With all of her fields bare now, she had no feed for her cows. She was able to buy one load of carrots, but she needed more. She told Ida, "My cows are in a mess."

Alice came to the ranch to help clean up. Helen called Mr. Kruger of the Alamo Lumber Company, and he came out and looked at the place. He told her it would cost about $800 to replace the windows and screens at the ranch house and José's house and the barn.

"I just wish Pell could have lived to see how his house held up in that storm, and saved his family."

CHAPTER SEVENTEEN

Carrie Lee's doctor ordered her to stop teaching because of her health problems, which he believed were life-threatening. He said she was suffering from nephritis and that at that time (1965) there was no cure for it. She did stop teaching. Her baby was a girl. They named her Alice Louise.

When the new baby was only a few weeks old, Robert came home from school to take her and Carrie Lee to the doctor in Falfurrias for a check-up, leaving the three older children at the ranch with Helen. The doctor found Carrie Lee in such critical condition that he told Robert to take her immediately to Spohn Hospital in Corpus Christi. On their way to the hospital, they stopped by Lou and Alice Hempel's house and left the baby with her aunt Alice.

Robert stayed at the hospital with Carrie Lee. When he went back to the ranch to get a change of clothes and Helen was cooking his breakfast, he told her something that they had been keeping from her. "He put his head down on the table and cried and told me Carrie Lee was going to die. I didn't believe it. But I went numb all over."

Robert took Helen and the children to see Carrie Lee. On the way they stopped by the Hempels' house and picked up baby Alice Louise and took her to the hospital with them. When Helen saw Carrie Lee, and touched her, she believed what Robert had told her was right. "She felt so cold."

While they were visiting, the nurses came and said Carrie Lee was to be transferred to Methodist Hospital in Houston, at once.

Helen just stood there. "She gave me her purse and told the children she had to go. They took her in a wheel chair to the elevator and she and Robert left. I wanted to run after the elevator. But I didn't. I went to the office and paid the bill. Then I took the baby to Alice and Lou, and the other children and I went back to the ranch. The next morning I opened her purse and found two letters: one to me,

CHAPTER SEVENTEEN

and one to her children. She already knew she was going to die, before we saw her that day. She asked Robert to give Alice Louise to Alice and Lou. He did, and they raised her as their own child."

To see this vibrant, headstrong, fun-loving child of hers have to die and leave a husband and four children while she was still in the prime of life was the most difficult thing Helen had ever had to face. But she did what she had to do—she took the three oldest children to live with her at the ranch. Robert was at the ranch when he could be, but he had to finish school and make a living. The responsibility rested heavily on Helen's sixty-nine-year-old shoulders. Meredith was five years old, Jennifer was seven, Robert Clyde was eight. Helen cared for them, sent them to school, took them to Sunday school, to parties, to the rodeo, disciplined them, treated them as if they were her own children. It was something to deal with—the responsibility, and the grief.

But her blithe spirit could not be completely crushed by sorrow and responsibility. By the summer of 1967 Carrie Lee had been gone two years, and Helen could write poetically to Ida: "It is daylight but the sun is not up yet. The air is damp and I hear many sounds. A mockingbird is trying to outsing some other bird. Yesterday the children found a bird's nest in the turkscap, full of blue eggs. I am weaning some calves and you can hear the cows bawling. I hear doves cooing in the distance, and hear the tractor getting ready to load silage. The mornings are pleasant, but as the day wears on Old Sol does his best to drive everything to the shade."

By July her spirits were low. She wrote again to Ida: "My last rain was the second of June. The drought still hangs on. The canícula [dog days] starts the 14th—I am afraid we are in for 40 more days of it."

And she said there was no activity in the oil business in Jim Hogg County. "With oil cut off from the Middle East it looks like the oil companies would get busy."

One of the brightest days in her summer was when she received a letter from Reginald, mailed from Ethiopia, telling her he was made chief scientist on the U.S. Coast and Geodetic Survey ship *Oceanographer* on several portions of the cruise from Massaua, Ethiopia, to Bombay, India, and from Bombay to Penang, Malaysia.

Helen had more than one reason to be happy when she received that letter. Not only was she pleased that her son had the honor to be named chief scientist, she felt lucky that the letter got to her at all, and that it brought news that Reginald was all right. It had taken it

Independence, Again

several weeks to reach her, because the 1967 Middle East War—which broke out after the *Oceanographer* left Massaua and ended before it reached Bombay—had disrupted mail and communications from that area. Reginald told his mother, "If the war had occurred two weeks earlier, we would have been trapped in the Suez Canal." It looked as if Reginald was meeting his own challenges. Helen didn't know whether to be proud or anxious.

She didn't have a lot of time to be either, in fact. There was never a dull moment at the ranch. Meredith, Jennifer, and Robert Clyde all came down with fever and earache. Helen felt sure their problems were caused by swimming in the stale water of the pila. "They *will* sneak off and go in there."

And Meredith was always coming up with ideas. Helen wrote to Ida: "I just happened to catch Meredith's reflection in the glass and saw her out there trying to lasso a calf. You have to watch them every minute. I don't think there was any danger of her roping it, but if by chance she got it I'd have to have someone catch the calf to take off the rope."

Robert and his three children spent the last part of the summer in Alpine. He attended Sul Ross University, and the children lived with their aunt Georgia and her family. Robert met and fell in love with a young lady from Waco who was also a student at Sul Ross that summer, and whom he later married. Her name was Barbara Steadman. She was a music major.

The last of July, Helen wrote to Hazel saying she thought the oil company would be drilling on her property soon, that she had seen a small plane flying slowly over the ranch "not much higher than my house."

She was correct. They did drill, and on the first of September they were putting the pump on the well. She told Ida she expected to sign the new lease that day. "We finally came to terms: I get $25.00 per acre, 1/16 over-riding royalty and a term of three years. This man said this company would not go for any over-riding royalty—but I got what I asked for. The company held back more on the time than anything. They wanted a five year lease. I learned in a round about way that this company is the Humble."

Georgia was having problems with her marriage. She and eleven-year-old Cynthia and six-year-old Martin, along with Robert's three children, came to the ranch that fall, and Georgia started teaching in

CHAPTER SEVENTEEN

Hebbronville. Helen had five grandchildren living at the ranch now. She told Ida that Martin and Meredith had played hard the last days before school started: "They leave the house to play at the troughs with tadpoles and only come in to eat."

There seemed to be no end to what Helen would undertake to do—and then *do*. She decided to remodel her house and add two rooms and a bath. "So I can have room for my children when they come home."

On January 4, 1968, she was ecstatic. She wrote to Ida: "I guess you wonder why my handwriting is so shaky. Well, when I get excited I do get trembly." Oil activity was what was causing all the excitement. "They finished well #3 last night—that is they set casing. Mr. Howard and Mr. Martin came by the house yesterday and brought me the log and compared it with no. 2."

And in that same letter she bragged: "Georgia had to make a poster for school last night. It was longer than my dining room table and also as wide. It represents the month of January. She really has the talent."

But on January 11 she was feeling low. She wrote to Ida again: "Do you remember that your Daddy used to say 'He that expecteth little, shall not be disappointed'? Well I thought of that yesterday when Mr. Teague came to tell me what potential my #2 well had on a 24-hour pump. It is 46 barrels per day. I knew they were not going to produce the well to full capacity, as it would soon ruin the well, but I had no idea they would cut it down that much. They think that is a good well—and maybe it is, but they will have to get several such wells to amount to something."

On January 20, 1968, Robert married Barbara. Helen told Hazel: "Barbara is a very lovely girl. She is sweet to the children and they are crazy about her." She said Barbara and Robert planned to take the children to live with them, that Barbara did not plan to teach during the spring semester but would teach again in the fall. Robert had been living at the Trap, and Helen, knowing he was not the best of housekeepers, sent Jesús and Rosa to clean the place before Barbara moved in.

Helen was pleased with Robert's marriage, and with things in general. She wrote to Hazel: "We have had many good rains, the country around here is beautiful. My cattle are fat." But her eternal optimism underwent much testing. And without another one of her attributes—bullheadedness—it might not have survived.

One particularly trying time was when the government inspector closed her dairy. He said the dairy barn needed to be painted, and he

Independence, Again

put her on probation for a couple of weeks to give her time to get it done. Helen went immediately and bought paint, but she couldn't find anybody to do the painting. She took Jesús out of the field, "where I needed him badly," and put him to painting the barn. He fell off the ladder and broke several ribs, and that stopped the painting. Helen tried frantically to find another painter. No luck. When the inspector came back, he ordered her to quit selling milk until the barn was painted. That put her in an impossible situation. What could she do with all that milk? She was selling between three and four thousand dollars' worth a month. If she poured it on the ground, it would create a health problem. Cotton Clark offered to haul it off for her and give it to a man who would feed it to his hogs.

She called the government field manager and complained about the predicament the inspector's decision placed her in. When nothing came of that, she called an auctioneer and told him to come and sell her dairy. "I hated to do it. I had so many fresh cows, and they were in good shape. But I was good and tired of dealing with that inspector. I made up my mind I would sell out at all costs and never again have such a thing to happen to me."

After arrangements were made for the auction, the inspector was sent to tell her she could start selling milk again, on a temporary basis, but he warned her, "I'll be back soon to check your barn."

Helen told him: "You don't need to ever come back again. I'm selling out right now!"

They had a big time the day of the sale. The auctioneer set up a large tent, and they ran the animals through one at a time. A couple of her friends had at one time worked at an auction barn, so they came and helped. The man ran the cattle through and his wife kept the records. The ladies from the Methodist Church in Hebbronville came out and set up a stand and sold sandwiches and coffee and cold drinks. This latter was at the suggestion of the auctioneer: "We don't want people leaving the auction and going off to get something to eat and not coming back."

There was a big crowd. People came from everywhere—Laredo, Falfurrias, Kingsville, Cotulla, Pearsall, San Antonio. Cars filled the dairy lot and the pasture in front of the house.

Helen was watching and enjoying it—until a government inspector from Rio Grande City showed up. He was a friend of her old adversary, the inspector she had been dealing with. He started telling her

CHAPTER SEVENTEEN

she wasn't getting enough money for the cows and the dairy equipment. "He wanted me to get crosswise with the auctioneer." She told him: "I've been to auctions around here. I know what things are selling for." And when he kept on badgering her about it, she tried to look at him the way she thought Pell would have, and then she turned her back on him and went in the house. "Boy! I'd had a belly full of government inspectors!"

Helen had mixed feelings about selling her dairy. A dairy is very confining. The person responsible for it feels tied to it every day, 365 days a year. Reginald had been trying for some time to get her to sell it, and there had been times when she had been almost willing to. This was not one of those times, however. "My pastures were green with grass, and my cows were giving lots of milk." The worst part was that now José Suarez and his family would have to move—José did not want to be a farmer. Helen hated to see them go. "They had a little home in Falfurrias, where they lived before he came to work for me, so they went back there. He had bought a second-hand car from me and still owed me about $300 on it. I canceled the note and gave him the car."

After the Suarezes left the ranch, Jesús and Rosa moved into the modern cinder-block house.

CHAPTER EIGHTEEN

Helen used the money from the sale of her dairy to stock the ranch with beef cattle, including twelve Black Angus heifers and a bull that she was very proud of.

Three-year-old Billy Luttrell saw a picture of some blue shoes and told his mother he wished they could buy them for Meemaw, so she could wear them and go dancing. Helen wrote to Ida: "I enjoyed your letter—especially the part where Billy wants to buy me some blue dancing shoes. I wish I could put some on and dance if it would make me feel young. I have been so sluggish lately."

She had driven alone to Alice a few days before and had gotten so sleepy she kept slapping herself on the head to try to stay awake. On the way home she even dozed off once, and a big watermelon truck passed and woke her up. She told Ida: "Old age is laying me on the shelf. I see every day I am getting more forgetful. I burned the beans up the other day. It makes me so mad."

But feeling older didn't seem to slow her down. In June the carpenters began to remodel her house, and she was "fighting like fire" to gather a bumper crop of feed before it burned up.

Robert was helping with the harvest. Barbara and the children came with him to the ranch on June 25, to celebrate Jennifer's birthday. It turned out to be a busy day. Early that morning Helen pushed the disorder of the remodeling out of her way and made Jennifer a German chocolate cake. After breakfast she went to Hebbronville to get a piece of the cane cutter welded. Then she called and rented a tractor, and took Robert to pick it up, and trailed along behind him on the way back "in case something failed."

The remodelers brought the cabinets for her new kitchen.

A truck brought a bulldozer to cover up the pit at the dry hole where the oil company had drilled her number 4 oil well.

CHAPTER EIGHTEEN

And the county chose that day to put in a new cattle guard and grade her road—in the midst of all that traffic.

A gravity meter crew that was surveying at the ranch that day told Helen they had seen a dead cow in the pasture, so she left the chaos at the house and went to check on her herd.

Ever with an eye for business, she talked the bulldozer operator into burying the dead cow and then cleaning out one of her silos while he was at the ranch: "It costs a lot if you have to have a dozer come out here for something—as it was, all I had to pay was $15.00."

So far, Helen's oil wells had not made her rich. All told, she had received $994 for oil, and $1,054 for the water used in drilling. The oil company apparently wasn't getting rich, either. One of the men told her they had spent over $100,000 on her lease.

In September, 1968, Helen's sister Opal died in Houston. Alleene and Garland were living at Wesley Manor in Weslaco at that time. Helen drove to Weslaco and went with Alleene to Houston by bus. Her daughter Ida met them, and she and Bill took them to Wharton to the funeral. Opal was the third Sewell sibling to die. Harold and Emil had both died within the last few years. "That was three of us gone. It left an empty feeling."

Her remodeling was finally completed, and she was eager to show off her nice house. September 21 she was hostess to the Women's Society of Christian Service. She invited several guests in addition to the members. In all, thirty ladies came. "They all raved about my house. I like it, too." And on November 25 she planned to entertain the Cenizo Garden Club. She told Hazel: "I'm going to have it out here. And I'm not only going to have the club members, but all the ex-members, and a few other guests besides."

The oil company asked for a ninety-day extension of the lease but didn't want to pay for it. Helen offered a forty-five-day extension if the company would cover the slush pit and bury the pipeline below plowing depth. But she asked for $350 if she gave them a ninety-day extension. They took the forty-five-day one.

December 7, 1968, Helen wrote to Ida: "Jesús quit Tuesday. He is going to work for that big outfit on Moody's. They will pay him $1.20 per hour. Isn't that neighborly of that outfit? I'm going to tell them what I think of them, too, hiring my farmer right under my nose!"

Jesús and Rosa moved to Hebbronville. His new employers planned

Independence, Again

to build a cinder-block house for him on the Moody ranch, but they rented a house in town for him, temporarily.

Helen went to Sejita to see her former employee Noé, to ask whether he knew any farmer she could hire. He promised to try to find somebody to bring her. Afterwards it occurred to her that Noé might bring her a man named Miguel who had at one time worked on the ranch. She told Ida: "He is a good farmer—but I'd hate to put up with Luisa and all those kids. She always made herself at home in my house. Rosa stays at her own house."

Jesús had been cutting feed when he quit. His departure left Helen in something of a bind. But it was not as bad as it might have been. She told Ida, "I am so thankful I don't have a dairy."

She needed a farmer. And Jesús was a good farmer. Every time she thought about those people enticing him away, her temperature went up. She was sitting by the window, writing to Ida. She told her: "I see Jesús out there now. He still has to take down his television antenna—and he said he would put the feed out for the cows this morning." And she told her, "Rosa was cleaning the house yesterday—that is more than some of them would do."

The thought of losing Jesús and Rosa was depressing. But a phone call from Reginald caused Helen's mood to change abruptly. He called to tell her he had been selected for *Who's Who in the East*. She wanted to dance and shout. She told Hazel, "Am I ever glad I got him out of that dairy barn!"

She hired a young couple to replace Jesús. She told her children: "The boy is just twenty years old, but he has worked four years with a tractor. They both speak good English. She graduated from high school last year. He went to the eighth grade."

If that young man had worked four years with a tractor, it didn't show. He didn't seem to know anything about machinery. He broke Helen's ensilage cutter the second day he used it. He had worked in the field only a few days when he broke one of the tractors. He couldn't get the plows to work on the other tractor. Helen told him to put the planter on and plant the corn, and he said the power lift wouldn't work. She sent to Falfurrias for a mechanic who came and got all the machinery in working order.

The next Saturday Helen, Georgia, Cynthia, and Martin went to Falfurrias. While they were gone, the young farmer was supposed to

CHAPTER EIGHTEEN

plant corn in the garden. When they came home, he hadn't planted it. He said the planter was broken.

Sunday morning Helen went to Hebbronville to find Jesús, to ask if he could come and fix the planter. He was not at home, but she talked with Rosa, and Rosa said she thought Jesús would like to come back and work for Helen. It had been three months since he quit. Rosa said he was not satisfied with the job with Helen's neighbor. She said he was paid by the hour, and when he couldn't work—when it rained, or when he was sick—he didn't get paid.

Later that morning, Helen's young farmer sent his wife to tell Helen he was quitting. He said he couldn't work there any more because he was always breaking things.

When Jesús came that afternoon to fix the planter, he and Helen sized each other up, trying not to show that each was eager for him to come back to work for her. Finally, she put the question to him directly. She told her children, "He acted like he needed some persuasion."

Helen and Jesús settled their differences, and he told her he would come back if she would pay him $55 per week. That was more than she had been paying the boy, but now she would get some farming done. Later she wrote to Ida: "You don't know what a relief it is to have Jesús back. He is the best farmer—not counting Bubs—that I ever had, and he knows how to take care of my cattle, too. I have gotten mad at him many times, but I'm going to try to get along with him."

In April the Cenizo Garden Club went on a field trip that was led by Warren Proctor, an agriculturist from the soil conservation office in Hebbronville. The club members took lunches and ate at the Robert Holbein ranch. Then they went out in the pastures, and Mr. Proctor pointed out the various kinds of grasses and explained how much feed per acre each kind would produce. Helen enjoyed that. "It got pretty hot, but one of the ladies had a parasol and she held it over me."

When it was time for the scholastic competition that spring, Helen went to school to hear the declamation contest. Jennifer won first place for fifth-grade girls. Helen told Ida: "She had such good poise and not afraid, she expressed herself well too. It made me think of Carrie Lee—she was so good in declaiming." Helen said she kept wishing Carrie Lee could have been there to hear Jennifer. "But Barbara was there, and she was just as proud."

On May 16, 1969, they got a good rain at the ranch. It started rain-

Independence, Again

ing in the northwest that afternoon. Helen watched the storm. "You never saw so much lightning. And it stayed in the same area for hours. I began to think it would never get here." She sat up late in order to see the weather on the ten o'clock news. "I wanted to watch the radar screen and see just where it was raining. I thought Carol Burnett's show would never end, but it did, and just as the news was ready to start the electricity went off. I hope God will forgive me for what I said." When the storm finally did break, it was severe. She had a rain gauge at the house that held five inches and one down in the field that held six. Both ran over. She said, "I guess that was part of my Mother's Day gift."

She learned that one of her neighbors was installing an irrigation system in his field. "They say one well with its irrigation pipes costs $100,000. That shows some people have faith in what this land can do."

That summer Helen had five grandchildren at the ranch most of the time. Barbara and Robert and his three children were living at the Trap, and Georgia and her two were living at the ranch. Helen taught Robert Clyde, Jennifer, and Cynthia to play Forty-two. She taught them to play, but she gave no quarter. Helen always played to win, no matter what the game was, or who the other players were.

She had two things to be excited about when she wrote to Hazel August 1. Her brother Howard had just been appointed superintendent at the Duval Sulphur Company in Orchard, Texas, where he had worked for several years. And she told Hazel she got a thrill out of watching the astronauts walking on the moon. "I wish Mama and Papa, and Pell and Carrie Lee could have seen it."

But by the time she was writing to Ida in January, 1970, she was having trouble finding something to be happy about. She had just learned that Alleene was having serious health problems. There had been a hard freeze at the ranch, and she had lost most of the plants in her garden. She had bought a new implement for digging ensilage, but it was not the one she had ordered and Jesús was not happy with it. And on top of that she was having trouble finding a place to write a letter. She had been working on her income tax and it was spread all over her bedroom. She'd had to fill out a report called "A Census of Agriculture" —answering pages of questions about the crops she grew last year, the cows and other animals she had, and on and on. "It gives me a headache! To write this letter I came to the kitchen." She ended the long letter of tribulations by telling Ida: "I shouldn't tell my troubles, but

CHAPTER EIGHTEEN

it lightens my tension to get it off my chest. Maybe the next time you hear from me it will be full of good cheer."

She watched the news on television every night. She particularly enjoyed keeping up with the astronauts. "I get all trembly over flights in space. I wish I could go up there."

But when she next wrote to Ida, her thoughts were earthbound. She was complaining of severe pain from arthritis. When the pain got so bad she couldn't sleep at night she went to see the doctor, and he had his nurse give her a shot. It didn't do much good. The next night she was up and down, so she finally just got up and swept her room and dressing room, and all the back part of the house. Then she mopped the kitchen. She hoped the exercise would get her blood circulating and maybe that would help. But it didn't. She sat down at the typewriter and tried to work on a couple of talks she was to give in the near future—one to the Cenizo Garden Club the next week entitled "How, When, and Where to Plant for Beauty," and one to the Self Culture Club in about a month on "Texas Heritage."

Hard as she tried, she could not ignore the pain, nor could she get rid of it. She was battling a formidable opponent, one that was as tenacious as she was. Maybe she couldn't win a clear victory, but she had no thought of going down in defeat. She was convinced that all it took was for her resolve to be greater than her pain. She later told a friend, "I didn't intend to let it keep me from doing what I wanted to do."

On August 21, 1971, two days after Helen's seventy-fifth birthday, Ida and Bill Luttrell's fourth child was born. They named him Richard. That made another grandchild for Helen to keep up with, and to be proud of.

In 1972 South Texas law enforcement officers from several departments were trying to stop the flow of marijuana and other illegal drugs across the Mexico-Texas border, just as in the early 1920s Pell and his fellow officers had tried to prevent the smuggling of illegal liquor. The semi-desert brush country of Jim Hogg County was still relatively sparsely settled in 1972; smugglers still found it easy to make their way through it without being seen.

In January the lawmen came to Helen and asked permission to set up a temporary camp at the Trap, from which they could monitor the back roads around Hebbronville. They said they had information about a shipment of drugs coming in through Brownsville and on up through Jim Hogg County. They put an antenna on top of the windmill at the

Independence, Again

Trap so they could talk with Brownsville, and they had a helicopter that they used for reconnaissance. Helen told her children: "It is exciting. Something like old times. I hope they catch them."

Her arthritis was getting worse. She told Ida she had inquired among her friends as to what it might cost to get a maid to help with the housework. One friend said she paid $1.25 per hour, plus $1.50 a day to cover car expenses to and from work. Helen told Ida: "I'm going to slow down. But guess I'll wait until after the district garden club show in Alice on March 16 and 17—I'm chairman of the horticulture section."

In September, 1972, Helen was using wetback labor to help build fence at the Trap. She and Jesús had tried, unsuccessfully, to find local men to help him. She told her children, "It is impossible to get help from Hebbronville because they are all on welfare and won't work." The young man who was renting the house and land at the Trap had gotten some wetbacks from the jail in Laredo, and he allowed Helen to use two of them. "It is legal to take them out to work for you, so long as you be sure to return them when you are through with them. I had to pay for them, and I had to feed them."

Every Sunday afternoon she stayed glued to the television and watched the football game. She learned the rules—knew them as well as any player. When the Cowboys made a mistake, she yelled at the television.

On December 22 she had two important things to do—she planned to meet her grandson Paul Bruce at the bus station at four o'clock in the afternoon, and she wanted to attend the important Christmas party Edith Armstrong was hosting at El Sordo for the members of the Cenizo Garden Club. She decided to try to do both. But by the time she left the party she was already late. She told Ida, "I buzzed my car to town—you know it buzzes when I drive it more than seventy-five miles an hour."

She arrived at the bus station after the bus did. Paul Bruce was waiting for her. He was neither surprised nor annoyed that she was late. She took him home and cooked his favorite dinner, including flour tortillas.

Her house was filled with children and grandchildren during the holidays. They ate a lot of flour tortillas and played a lot of Forty-two. Come January she was alone again, as Georgia and her children were living in an apartment in Hebbronville that winter.

Early in January, 1973, there was a bad ice storm at the ranch. For

CHAPTER EIGHTEEN

two or three days Helen had no electricity, no heat, no water, and no telephone. Jesús made her a good fire in the fireplace, and she cooked breakfast there. Georgia brought a pot roast and other hot food. Earnest and Edith Armstrong came to check on her. They were on their way to Laredo to stay at a hotel until the utility services were restored at their ranch. They tried to get Helen to go with them, but she declined. "I wanted to stay at home."

The ice storm and the inconveniences it caused were not the worst of Helen's problems. There was one she tried not to think about—didn't even want to talk about. "Every time I think about it I get shook up." William Greesenbeck, the young man who had been renting the Trap, had come and told her that the house at the Trap burned to the ground. She had fixed it up only a few months ago for William and his bride. He said they were in Hebbronville at his father-in-law's house when the misfortune occurred. All their new furniture and all their wedding gifts burned with the house. And they didn't have any insurance. William asked whether Helen wanted him to take her over to see the place. She said, "No. I don't even want to look at it."

Garland's health had been poor for several years. She died the last of February, 1973. It was not a shock to Helen because she had known Garland could not live long. She had been expecting it. But it left a painful void, nevertheless. They had been especially close all their lives: "There is a loneliness."

Myrtle Draper and her son Alfred came to see Helen after Garland's death. The Drapers and the Sewells had stayed close friends ever since the Sewell girls were children—when the Drapers lived at Santa Rita and the Sewells lived at Tipperary. But Myrtle was crippled by arthritis now and was living in Houston to be near Alfred and his family. She had come to Hebbronville to sell some property, and had come by to see Helen. They had to visit in Alfred's car because Myrtle did not wish to try to walk the short distance from the car to the house. Helen had been lying down when they arrived, because she, too, was having trouble with arthritis. "Myrtle and I are both old crippled ladies now. We used to have such good times together. That was a long time ago."

In March of that year Helen told Ida: "I have made up my mind to do something about my legs and hips. So yesterday I went to see Dr. Glendenning and told him I wanted him to put some cortisone under my knee caps and also put some in my hip. I'm going to get myself in shape so I can walk around and see the flowers when you

Independence, Again

and I go to Bellingrath Gardens [in Mobile, Alabama]. I am supposed to show my garden April 10. I can go to Bellingrath anytime it suits you after that."

It had been a long time since Helen had seen any of the Presnall family with whom she lived when she was in high school in Alice, though they stayed in touch. In March, 1974, she received a letter from Julia Presnall Cage, inviting her to come to lunch at the Cage ranch out from Falfurrias. Julia said her mother would be there. Helen was delighted, especially with the prospect of a visit with Mrs. Presnall. Afterwards, she wrote to her children: "Mrs. Presnall is eighty-seven years old now. She was as happy to see me as I was to see her. We talked a lot about the years gone by."

Helen often had some of her family, especially her grandchildren, at the ranch. In the summer of 1974 Hazel, her son Paul Bruce, and Paul Bruce's friend Tommy were visiting there. Helen, the two boys, and Meredith played Forty-two until eleven o'clock or later almost every night.

The grandchildren usually worked when they were at the ranch. Martin and Meredith helped Jesús round up cattle and take two loads of calves to the auction. Helen and all the young people went the next day to watch the calves sell.

Helen wrote to Ida and said she had heard that her friend Mary Presnall Wise had a plastic joint put in her hip. Helen said she was thinking she might have the joints replaced in her knee and her hip. She asked Ida to check into the procedure there in Houston, and she told her: "But I want to get everything in order here before I do it, so if I should die in surgery you children won't have to worry about things. My lawyer tells me that land is selling for around $300.00 an acre. But I want to have plenty of heifers on hand, because cattle are a lot easier to liquidate than land if you need money for settling an estate or something. Then if you need money to replace them you can get a chattel mortgage. Most ranchers do have chattel mortgages on their cattle. I don't. I don't owe any money on anything. That is how I want to keep it."

By June, 1975, Helen's arthritis was so bad she was using a wheelchair. In fact, she killed a rattlesnake once, with her cane, while she was in the wheelchair. "It wasn't a very big one. I killed it on the porch."

But arthritis or no arthritis, she could go into ecstasy over a good rain. She told Ida: "I wound up with a little over three inches! This

CHAPTER EIGHTEEN

country can come back quicker than any I ever saw. I now have my cattle in the fields of hay grazer. My milo maize has made so much progress since the rains that I might be able to harvest it after all—I don't know how that crop kept alive, with no rain for so long. I even have nice roasting ears now. I got Jesús to put some in my deep freeze."

Robert Clyde came to help Jesús vaccinate and brand. And he planned to stay and help with the planting, which was late that year because they did not have enough moisture to plant earlier. They had to plant after a rain, when the soil was damp enough to make the seeds germinate. No rain, no planting.

Helen wrote to Ida: "We all went to Kingsville for Robert Clyde's high school graduation. I didn't take my wheelchair, but I surely wished I had it after I got there."

In the same letter she said: "Alice says she and Alice Louise are coming to the ranch to celebrate Alice Louise's birthday under the old Lemonade Tree where you children used to have your birthday parties."

And she told her: "Tell Anne I'm so very proud of her for winning the award in creative writing. And tell Billy how proud I am of him for winning second place in math."

In October, 1975, Helen told Ida: "I'm ready to have a plastic joint put in my knee. Find me a surgeon there in Houston, and make the arrangements."

CHAPTER NINETEEN

Replacing a knee joint turned out to be more of an ordeal than Helen anticipated. After the operation she stayed in Houston with Ida and her family until she was strong enough to travel back to the ranch. Hazel then came and stayed at the ranch until Helen could get along by herself. By that time Helen was walking, with some pain. The pain didn't stop her, though.

Two months after her operation she wrote to Ida, saying she had to type the letter instead of writing by hand because she didn't have the proper control over the muscles in her hand. She had been to see the doctor. "He says I'm OK." And after her appointment with the doctor she had gone to the hairdresser's. "When I got home I was exhausted. I am impatient to get back to normal."

Back to normal or not, she obviously was in control at the ranch. She told Ida she had bought two Charolais bulls since she came home.

Another piece of news was that Martin and Robert Clyde had seen a cougar at the Trap.

In May, 1976, Helen wrote to Ida about a problem, and a solution: "My left leg has been swollen. Day before yesterday my foot was so swollen I had a difficult time getting on my shoe. Georgia tried to get me to go to the doctor, but when I think of sitting there in his waiting room for hours I can find many excuses for not going. So I decided to do something about the swelling myself. I doubled the diuretic pills and on top of that I started to take some Doan's pills and that took the swelling out and I feel a lot better."

Jennifer would graduate from high school in Kingsville in less than a month, and Helen wanted to go to her graduation. "That's why I got busy and got that swelling out of my foot."

In July Helen wrote to her children: "Jennifer has obtained $2500.00 in grants for college. She will have to work for $800.00 of it, but that is good. Barbara took her to Austin on Monday, for orientation."

CHAPTER NINETEEN

Meredith wanted to enter the rodeo competition in Hebbronville, and she needed thirty dollars. Helen reported, "I paid her for her pig, so she could have her entrance fee." Meredith did exceptionally well. The next morning the school bulletin board said in big letters: "HHS salutes Meredith Anderson, our bronc rider!" But Helen was concerned about Meredith. She told Ida: "I think she's in love. I told her she had better not get serious, that she still has two years of high school and four years of college. Doesn't this remind you of Carrie Lee? It's too bad her mother could not have seen her ride the bronc."

Another thing about Meredith that reminded Helen of Carrie Lee was her way with animals. One Sunday afternoon, right after Meredith had taken a bath and washed her hair and put on clean clothes—"she looked so pretty"—Martin came in and said the sow was ready to have pigs. So away she went to the pig pen. Helen told Ida: "They say a sow is real mean when she has pigs, and will attack anyone who gets in the pen. But Meredith climbed right in that pen and gave the sow a drink of water and helped her deliver all thirteen pigs. She even ran to the house bringing me the first that was born—a little white and black spotted pig. Martin stayed on the outside and would hand her a rag every time one was born, and she would wipe the mucus off its nose. Jesús said Meredith really worked with that sow. The sow started having these pigs before sundown and those kids stayed with her until after ten o'cock."

Meredith called Robert Morris, the agriculture teacher at the high school, to ask what to do with the pigs that night. "He said to do what Jesús said; take the pigs away from her so she could not mash them." They made a house of hay bales and covered them up so nothing could get them.

"One thing I didn't need was more pigs!"

Martin was at the ranch at that time because he planned to help Jesús fill the silo that week. All of Helen's grandsons worked at the ranch when they could. Martin killed a javelina at the Trap while he was there.

On July 21 Helen wrote to Ida: "About you and Hazel planning a birthday party for me, just forget that—I'm not going to send you any list of names. I don't want a party, I just want my own children here. Edith had that big party for me last year, and I'd be embarrassed to invite my friends to another birthday party."

Alice called Helen and told her that an independent oil operator

Independence, Again

from Missouri told her and Lou he was interested in leasing the Harbison ranch for oil, and he wanted Helen to call him. Helen told her, "You tell him to call *me*."

In September, 1976, less than a year after she had a plastic joint put in her knee, she told Ida she was ready for her to make her an appointment to have her hip joint replaced. She said anytime in October would be fine. And she told Ida not to worry about getting somebody to stay with her after the operation, that with the wheelchair she could take care of herself. She said Rosa couldn't help because she had little Deside to look after, but that Jesús would help her—she didn't need anybody else.

She felt sure this operation would not be as major as the one she had on her knee, saying that the doctor told her a person could almost walk away from a hip-joint operation. And she declared she was through taking shots: she said the last time she took one she had to wait and wait, and then the nurse hit a vein. "I'm not going to take any more of those shots. You always lose so much time in the doctor's office."

On October 28 she went to a hospital in Houston and had a plastic joint put in her hip, and by November 17 she was back at the ranch. Hazel was with her. Helen wrote to Ida and Bill: "I miss all of you. You don't know how much I appreciate all you did for me. You, Bill, and the children were all so thoughtful of me. And now Hazel is here, and she is working like a Turk. Right now she is scouring and cleaning my bathroom. She never stops."

November 29 Helen drove her car for the first time since her hip operation. "It was good to get back under the wheel. It had been a whole month."

By January, 1977, she was in a mood to get rid of her hogs. She never did care much for hogs, anyway. She had two sows, several half-grown pigs, and a boar. She told Jesús and Martin to load them all up and take them to the auction. Martin told her he had heard that the auction in Hebbronville wasn't selling hogs any more. She ignored him and told them to load the hogs. Hogs are hard to load, but they finally got them in the trailer. Before they started with them, she decided to call and ask what they were selling for. To her amazement, Martin was right—the auction did not sell hogs. Well, she would send them to another auction. She started calling. Nobody was selling hogs. Finally, she found an auction in Alice that said they sold hogs. Good. She had

CHAPTER NINETEEN

won. But . . . they held the auction only on Tuesdays. And this was Thursday. So the hogs had to be unloaded.

The next day one of the sows had ten pigs! Helen was exasperated. She couldn't send pigs that young to the auction. She would have to keep that sow and those pigs for another few weeks. "I never was so sick of pigs in my whole life."

But if she was annoyed with her hogs, she was delighted with her cattle. In February she sent ten calves and a bull to the auction and received 39.75 cents a pound for some of them. "I knew the price would go up after Jimmy Carter got in. That's why I voted for him."

The Brooks County Hospital in Falfurrias needed volunteers to help in the office, and some of Helen's friends from Hebbronville were planning to work over there one or two days a month. They wanted Helen to volunteer also. She told Ida: "I am too impatient to sit there at a desk all day. Besides, I am eighty years old and I have a full time job with my ranch, my housework and yard and garden. There are a lot of women in Falfurrias that don't do anything but play bridge. I still have to tell them I can't do it."

In March, 1977, Helen and Jesús were having a disagreement, and she said she was going to replace him. Rosa came and cried and said she didn't want to move. She told Helen: "When Deside gets to be three years old I will come and work for you." And she told her: "When we told Aidé we might move to town she said she wouldn't go, that she would stay with Meemaw. And when we told her you were not her real grandmother she cried and didn't want to believe it."

Helen told Ida, "If Jesús didn't get so darn independent with me, I'd just keep them."

In a letter to Ida she said that a man with a canning company in Tyler had called her, trying to interest her in a program for planting purple hull peas. She said she had learned from Robert Morris that the company was considered to be reliable; some farmers already had contracts with it. And she told her: "The company contracts the farmer to plant a certain number of acres and agrees to pay him so much per pound for the seed. This is the biggest pea-canning company in Texas, has been in business for seventy years. They will see to it that we get a combine when the peas are mature. The crop puts nitrogen into the soil and will mature in around seventy days. I could plant another crop such as Chinese peas later in the fall. I sure would like to, but if it doesn't rain I can't plant anything."

Independence, Again

At the end of the letter she added, "I have decided to keep Jesús."

In May she wrote to Ida regarding an article called "A Basket of Gold," which Ida had written about Helen, and also regarding a children's book that Ida was trying to market. She told her: "I believe you will go far with your writing. It takes a lot of patience and perseverance, but once you have published one book it will be easier to publish the next one."

Helen was accustomed to leasing her land for bird hunting, but she never did lease any of it for deer hunting. "I keep that for my grandchildren." She even allowed them to plant a few acres of oats or grass to entice the deer. In June of 1977 Martin took the tractor to the Trap and broke five acres. "He wants to plant hay grazer for the deer."

By now Helen was no longer using ensilage as feed for her cows. It had become impractical. She was using hay, stored in round bales. According to Reginald, "They put those large round bales in the field and let the cows feed from them. It is more wasteful, and it is not as good as ensilage. But even with modern equipment, storing and feeding ensilage is no longer cost efficient."

Jim Hogg and the surrounding counties were suffering a drought in the spring of 1978. Helen sent six calves to the auction and, as was her custom, went to watch them sell. She didn't stay very long—it was not a pleasant place to be that day. Zapata, Starr, and Webb counties had gotten even less rain than Jim Hogg County, and cattle there "were dying like flies." Many of the cows at the auction were pitifully poor, so weak they could hardly walk. Some would fall and couldn't get up. Helen left before her calves sold. "I couldn't look any more."

The night of May 2 Helen got the first rain she'd had in some time. She said she slept only one hour that night—it was thundering, and she was so eager for it to rain she couldn't relax. It started raining softly about four o'clock, and she drifted off to sleep. She awakened at five and "just couldn't wait to see the rain gauge." It had rained three-fourths of an inch. "We needed it so desperately."

In August, 1979, Helen went to Alice to attend her high school reunion. She told her children: "I got to see a few of my old friends, but was saddened by the news of some having too bad health to attend. Alice Presnall has cancer again, and there is no cure for her. Thelma Pearce is very crippled and has to use a walker. Hortense Lynn died a short time ago. It was when her first child was born that I went to Alice to help her, and then stayed on and went to high school. When

CHAPTER NINETEEN

you see all your friends passing on you realize that life on earth is very short."

When they got in line for lunch that day, a man Helen knew, and who was near the head of the line, filled his plate and came and wanted to give it to her. "I didn't want to take it, but I did, because he was insisting and I didn't want to draw so much attention to myself.

"And then some of the ladies in charge made Mrs. Hayes and me come to the table where the cake was being served, and have our pictures taken. I was the only one from the 1917 class that was there. I was the oldest graduate."

Reginald had been trying to persuade Helen to go to Hawaii with him and Beverly that fall, but she had been reluctant to try such a long trip. She told him, "I'm too old and trembly."

She was still facing challenges, though, and still finding them spirit-stirring. One day she had taken a hoe and gone to her garden to chop a few weeds, but she had found so many she was exhausted and shaky by the time she finally stopped and started making her way wearily toward the house. As she passed a Ponderosa lemon tree in the yard, she heard the familiar warning of a rattlesnake. She could not see the snake, but she knew it was there, somewhere in the grass and weeds under the tree. She also knew she didn't have the strength to kill it with a hoe, tired as she was.

She was alone at the ranch that day—Jesús and Rosa had gone to Falfurrias. She went in the house and called the Armstrong ranch—if Earnest was at home, he would come and kill the snake. But the Armstrongs did not answer. Well, she was on her own. If she got that snake, she would have to do it by herself.

She got her shotgun out of the closet. She had not tried to use it for more than a year because she had considered that her hands and arms were not steady enough to aim a gun. She didn't know whether she had any ammunition, but she did find one shell, in the drawer where she kept her recipes.

She loaded the gun and went outside and looked for the snake. She threw a rock under the lemon tree, but got no response. She circled a bed of phlox, and then she saw him, crawling toward a row of hedge. She knew if he reached that, he would get away, so she raised her gun and shot. She missed. The snake started crawling back in the opposite direction, toward a clump of lantana.

She went in the house and looked for another shell, and did find

Independence, Again

one, back in the corner of the drawer, behind some old recipes. She loaded her gun again and went back out in the yard. She threw a water sprinkler into the lantana, but got no answer. She moved to the shade of a live oak tree to get away from the glare, and then she saw him, coiled among some rocks over there. She braced herself against the tree, took aim as carefully as she could, and fired.

"I shot him to pieces, he didn't even have a chance to rattle."

The next day she went to town and bought herself a box of shells.

And then she wrote to Reginald and Beverly and told them, "I have decided to go to Hawaii with you, anytime you are ready."

On the way, they spent a couple of days in San Francisco seeing the city and the area around the bay by tour bus. Helen told her other children that all of it was enjoyable, but she complained: "We passed by a big conservatory of flowers but the bus did not stop there—that was what I wanted to see."

She was excited about Hawaii. "I have seen some frangipani (*Plumeria*) as big as trees, and in all colors!" She said she was having a wonderful time. "Bubs is so good to take care of all the travel arrangements. And Beverly is so good to look out for me."

Evidently the fields her grandsons planted to attract the deer were having their effect. "Jesús and Martin see deer in my oat fields all the time now, eating with the cattle. The first thing I know they will be crowding out my cows. Jesús saw ten yesterday. The boys like to hear that."

In January she was getting ready to talk to the Cenizo Garden Club about bulbs, and later to lead the "Call to Prayer and Self Denial" at the church.

She was reading various books she had received for Christmas. One was J. Frank Dobie's *Cow People*. She told her children, "I'm enjoying reading about all those ranch characters."

She wrote to Ida's son Billy, to thank him for his Christmas gift. And she told him that she and Martin had been down in the oats field the day before and had seen a big bunch of curlews. She said her father used to kill them, but she thought they were "off limits for shooting" now. She told Billy, "They are good to eat, and are much bigger than a dove or quail."

She apparently was catching up on her overdue correspondence, because she wrote to Ida's son Richard that same day. "I'm so proud of you for making that little car, and winning fourth place." She added:

CHAPTER NINETEEN

"I ran across this picture of a little brown thrush, and I thought you might like it. It reminds me of a song we sang at school when I was a very small girl. Let's see if I can remember it." And she typed the words:

> There's a Little Brown Thrush
> Sitting up in a tree, he's singing
> to you and he's singing to me.
> What does he say, little girl, little boy?
> "Oh the world is running over with joy.
> Now I'm glad, now I'm free and I always
> shall be, unless you bring sorrow,
> bring sorrow to me."

In January, 1983, Helen passed another big milestone in her life. She sold her cattle and got out of ranching. It had been fifty-four years since she and Pell started operating the ranch. And exactly half of that time Helen had been operating it by herself.

She planned to continue living in her poured-concrete house. But she leased her land for grazing. Life would be very different for her now. She did not need a man for farming or to care for cattle. Jesús and Rosa and their two little girls moved to town. He told her he would still come back and do odd jobs for her when she needed somebody.

When it was time to take the test for renewal of her driver's license, he came and took her to town. She passed it.

In March the Cenizo Garden Club had a flower show, and Helen won ten blue ribbons and the grand sweepstakes award. It was not anything unusual—she had been winning top awards for her flowers and her arrangements ever since she joined the club right after Pell died. She almost always won more ribbons than anybody else when she entered a show. And when she won a red instead of a blue, she vowed she'd win the blue next time.

Besides her many local awards, she had, over the years, been honored by various district and national garden club organizations. In 1960 District Seven of Texas Garden Clubs presented her with a Certificate of Award as Garden Citizen of the Year. And in 1982 the National Council of State Garden Clubs presented her with a Certificate of Commendation for long service as a member of the Cenizo Garden Club.

Several times she was offered the presidency of the Cenizo Garden Club, but she always refused. "I was selfish to say no. But it would

Independence, Again

have taken me away from my flowers more than I would like. My hunger for flowers sometimes makes me piggish."

Somewhat later that spring Helen was in the hospital in Corpus Christi, with erysipelas. She had an acute case, with extremely high fever, and the doctors and her children feared for her life. But her spirit was not diminished. Once, when a young doctor was at her bedside and was evidently searching for something cheerful to say, he asked her, "Where did you get those eyes of blue?"

Helen looked at him and quipped, "Out of the sky, as I was passing through."

The doctor, obviously taken aback, looked at Ida and raised his eyebrows.

After she was back at the ranch she wrote to Ida and Bill, thanking them for taking care of her at their home when she came out of the hospital, and for allowing Billy to drive her back to the ranch: "Robert Clyde came the day Billy left. And Martin will probably be here about the time Robert Clyde has to go. It is nice to have grandsons."

In May she was preparing to host a meeting of the United Methodist Women, although she was still weak from her bout in the hospital. She told her children: "Rosa is coming Thursday morning to clean up. And Jesús will help me too. Also, Robert Clyde is here. He is very good in helping me. He even cooks the meals sometimes. And he always washes the dishes."

In November she told Ida: "Another one of my pictures came out in the Laredo paper. This time I had my mouth shut, and the picture was not quite as bad as the last one. However, it tells me I'm getting old. I know it. I can feel it."

But her actions belied her words. In that same newspaper she found a story about a man who was growing apples in South Texas, something that was not supposed to be possible because of the lack of cool weather. Well. Here was a new challenge. She told Ida: "The variety is *Elah*. See if you can find me a couple of those trees in one of the nurseries in Houston."

In August, 1984, she wrote to Ida: "Dagma [Dagmar Gruy Cole] is having a fandango Saturday evening. I hope I'm feeling able to attend. Not that I can dance. But I would like to hear the music and watch the dancing."

Helen regained her health, to an extent. But the doctor told her and

CHAPTER NINETEEN

her children that she now had a very serious heart condition, and he suggested that she carry a cane. She did carry one from then on—part of the time. When she left it behind, her children and friends were never sure whether it was an accident or a purposeful act. One thing was sure—if her physical strength lacked something, her spirit was intact.

One day a couple of young birdwatchers came to the ranch hoping to see curlews. She offered to go out with them. When they started toward their station wagon, Helen walked toward her own car. She told them, "We'll take my car—I know how not to get stuck in the sand."

And one day in the spring of 1985, when a friend had driven down from Austin to go with Helen to a party on one of the other ranches that afternoon, Helen met her at the door, ready to go. As they left the house the friend said, "The car is at the front."

Helen said, "We're taking my car, and I'm driving. You're tired." And that was how it was. People seldom argued with Helen.

One day when several of her children and a friend were at the ranch, Helen was congratulating one of her daughters for an accomplishment, and then she turned to the friend and said, "She's talented."

That prompted Reginald to tease Helen by remarking to the friend: "Do you know why everybody in Hebbronville believes the Harbison kids are smart? Mother tells them so!"

Near the end of September Helen fell in her home and broke a hip. She was taken to Doctors Hospital in Laredo.

She told her children and the doctors: "I've been contemplating having a plastic joint put in this hip, anyway, like the one I have in the other hip. Now that I'm here, I think we might as well go ahead and do that, so I don't have to come back."

The doctors did not agree. In fact, they considered that her heart very likely would not stand any kind of operation, so they didn't even put a pin in the hip for several days—and they did it then largely because she insisted that they get it over with. "I was getting tired of that place."

By the first of November she was back at the ranch, learning to walk again.

On November 23, 1985, she prepared her quarterly income tax report and wrote a couple of letters that she instructed Georgia to mail the next day. She also telephoned several of her children and a few friends. She was excited about a big Christmas party that was being planned

CHAPTER NINETEEN

for the Cenizo Garden Club's December meeting at the Armstrong ranch. She was trying to persuade an East Texas friend to drive down for the party.

That night she died in her sleep.

Another long funeral procession wound through the little town.

As people left the graveside, someone was heard to say, "She was always herself—without apology."

BIBLIOGRAPHY

The sources I used in writing this story are primary, as described in the Acknowledgments and the Preface. But I found published material that was helpful in establishing background and perspective, and I list some of those publications below. I believe anyone wishing to read further about the way of life in South Texas during the late nineteenth and early twentieth centuries should find them interesting.

Allen, John Houghton. *Song to Randado.* Dallas: Kaleidograph Press, 1935. A group of poems describing the area around Randado and Hebbronville, and the men who worked the herds there.

Dobie, J. Frank. *A Vaquero of the Brush Country, Partly from the Reminiscences of John Young.* Boston: Little, Brown, 1952. 302 pp. illus. What life was like for the men who herded cattle in South Texas in the early days.

―――. *The Longhorns.* Boston: Little, Brown, 1941. 388 pp. index. illus. by Tom Lea. The story of Texas Longhorn cattle and their influence on South Texas.

Durham, George, as told to Clyde Wantland. *Taming the Nueces Strip: The Story of McNelly's Rangers.* Austin: University of Texas Press, 1962. 178 pp. illus. Deals with the unlawful conditions that existed in the area between the Nueces River and the Rio Grande in the last half of the nineteenth century.

Fisher, O. C., with J. C. Dykes. *King Fisher: His Life and Times.* Norman: University of Oklahoma Press, 1966. 157 pp. bibliog. The story of a notorious character set against the lawlessness of the Nueces Strip during the last half of the nineteenth century.

Gilliland, Maude T. *Rincon.* Brownsville, Texas: Springman-King Lithograph Company, 1964. 105 pp. illus. Autobiography. Interesting detail about growing up on a very large, isolated ranch in Starr and Hidalgo counties in the early 1900s.

Bibliography

———. *Horsebackers of the Brush Country.* Brownsville, Texas: Springman-King Lithograph Company, 1968. 175 pp. bibliog. index. Chapters about individual Texas Rangers. One chapter on Pelton Bruce Harbison, husband of Helen Sewell Harbison.

Jackson, Jack. *Los Mesteños.* College Station: Texas A&M University Press, 1986. 704 pp. bibliog. index. illus. Excellent source material about Spanish and Mexican ranches and ranching in Texas, 1721–1821. Nice illustrations.

Lasater, Dale. *Falfurrias: Ed C. Lasater and the Development of South Texas.* College Station: Texas A&M University Press, 1985. 296 pp. illus. index. bibliog. The development, by Anglos, of large ranches in South Texas, and the sale of isolated, semidesert land to naïve northerners, in the late 1800s and early 1900s.

Mitchell, Quita, ed. *Jim Hogg County 50th Anniversary.* Hebbronville, Texas: Jim Hogg County Chamber of Commerce, 1963. 160 pp. illus. Many old photographs of people and their activities. Several journals written by people who lived in that area in the early 1900s. Names of county officials, from when the county was first formed in 1913 to 1963.

Peavey, John R. *Echoes from the Rio Grande, 1905 to Now.* Brownsville, Texas: Springman-King Lithograph Company, 1963. 320 pp. illus. Mr. Peavey was a customs agent. Excellent detail about way of life in South Texas during the first part of the twentieth century.

was composed into type on a Compugraphic digital phototypesetter in twelve point Bembo with one point of spacing between the lines. University Roman was selected for display. The book was designed by Jim Billingsley, typeset by Metricomp, Inc., printed offset by Thomson-Shore, Inc., and bound by John H. Dekker & Sons. The paper on which the book is printed carries acid-free characteristics for an effective life of at least three hundred years.

TEXAS A&M UNIVERSITY PRESS
College Station

www.ingramcontent.com/pod-product-compliance
Lightning Source LLC
Chambersburg PA
CBHW031242290426
44109CB00012B/403